The SIX BASIC DOCTRINES
of Christianity

Dirk Waren

The SIX BASIC DOCTRINES of Christianity

Copyright © 2019 by Dirk Waren

All rights reserved. No original part of this book may be reproduced or transmitted in any form or by any means, electronic or mechanical, including photocopying, recording, or by any information storage and retrieval system, without the written permission of the Publisher, except where permitted by law.

Unless otherwise indicated, all Scripture quotations are taken from the Holy Bible, New International Version®. NIV®. Copyright © 1973, 1978, 1984, 2011 by the International Bible Society. Used by permission of Zondervan Bible Publishers.

Many NIV citations are from the 2011 Revised edition.

Other translations are listed in the Bibliography.

All underlining, italics and bracketed notes in scriptural citations are added by the author.

Pronominal references to Deity in this work are not always capitalized.

Edited by KEEII.

ISBN: 978-0-578-58437-9
PUBLISHED BY SOARING EAGLE PRESS
Youngstown

Printed in the United States of America

Therefore let us move beyond the elementary teachings about Christ and be taken forward to maturity,
- Hebrews 6:1

CONTENTS

Establishing a Firm FOUNDATION 9
    The Six Basic Doctrines 10

1. REPENTANCE from Acts that Lead to Death 13
    "Keeping with Repentance" 15
    Repentance from Dead Works 16
    Summary 17

2. FAITH in God 18
    Faith for Salvation & Eternal Life 20
    Everyone has Faith, but Not Necessarily Faith in God 20
    Repentance and Faith 21
    Repentance and Faith are Not Works 23
    The New Covenant is a Covenant of FAITH 24
    Faith *and* Perseverance (Patience) 24
    Faith *IN* GOD 25
    Faith in God, not Faith in Faith 26
    How Does Faith Grow? 27

3. Instructions about BAPTISMS 29
    Baptism into Christ 30
    Water Baptism 30
    Baptism of the Holy Spirit 31
    The Empowerment and Help of the Holy Spirit 35
    Power 36
    Love 38
    Self-control 43

4. The Laying on of Hands 48
    Blessing (or General Prayer) 48
    Anointing/Separation for Ministry 49
    The Holy Spirit Baptism 50
    Healing and Spiritual Deliverance 50

Important Points on Transmitting the Anointing 51

5. The RESURRECTION of the Dead 54
The Resurrection of the Righteous 56
Why is it called the "First Resurrection"? 58
'Isn't this Too Complicated?' 61
Jesus' Rapture of the Church and Return to Earth 63
"For it will Not be, Unless the Departure Comes First" 73

6. Eternal JUDGMENT 78
The Great White Throne Judgment: Eternal Judgment of the Lost 79
The Judgment Seat of Christ 83
Appraising the Believer's Works at the Judgment Seat 89
Penalties for Believers at the Judgment Seat vs. Reaping the Wages of Sin for Fakes 94
You Won't Often Hear Ministers Teach These Passages 97
Concluding Words on the Judgment Seat 99
The Sheep and Goat Judgment 101
Proof that the Sheep and Goat Judgment Applies to Living Non-Christians at the End of the Tribulation 105
What is the Sheep and Goat Judgment All About? 106
The Salvation Equation 110
The "Sheep" Who Are Allowed to Enter the Millennium 113
"Produce FRUIT in keeping with repentance" 114
Another Example of Misapplying the Sheep and Goat Judgment 117
The False Prophets of Matthew 7:15-23 and the Judgment Seat of Christ 119
The Judgment of Old Testament Saints 120

7. ETERNAL LIFE 122
A New Earth and Universe 122
Will We "Spend Eternity in Heaven"? 123
The New Jerusalem will come "Down out of Heaven from God" 125
Between Physical Death and Bodily Resurrection 126
Quality of Life in the New Earth and Universe 128
There will be Nations and Kings on the New Earth 132
The Entire Universe will be Under Humanity's Control 136

Where the Error Started 141
The Coming Universal Utopia 143
"The Final Restoration of All Things" 144
What's the Purpose of the Millennium? 146
Conclusion on the Final Restoration of All Things 147
Eternity and Your Beloved Pets 149
Are You Looking Forward to Eternal Life? 150

Conclusion 151

Bibliography 153

8

Introduction

Establishing a Firm FOUNDATION

Establishing a sound spiritual **foundation** is important because it sets the groundwork for the believer's entire walk with the Lord. Just as a good foundation is a prerequisite for a sound building, so a proper spiritual foundation is vital for an effective, liberating and victorious Christian life. People who fail to lay a proper foundation are doomed to spiritual immaturity because they have nothing by which to judge what is right or wrong, scriptural or unscriptural, appropriate or inappropriate, wise or foolish. Simply put, **a healthy biblical understructure eliminates feeble spirituality**.

Believers who fail to establish a good foundation can shipwreck their faith altogether, as Paul put it in 1 Timothy 1:19, and find themselves back in the world—in spiritual darkness and separate from God. That's why this book exists. It'll help believers lay a quality understructure so that their faith isn't shipwrecked at some point down the road.

The Six Basic Doctrines

Many Christians don't know this, but the Bible details six doctrines that will ensure a sound spiritual foundation:

> **Therefore let us move beyond the elementary teachings about Christ and be taken forward to maturity, not laying again <u>the foundation</u> of repentance from acts that lead to death, and of faith in God, ² instruction about baptisms, the laying on of hands, the resurrection of the dead, and eternal judgment.**
>
> **Hebrews 6:1-2**

The writer of Hebrews was lamenting that the believers he was addressing needed to be taught these basic doctrines all over again when they should've been teachers by this point (see Hebrews 5:11-12). Notice that knowing these six elementary doctrines is spoken of in terms of "laying" a "foundation." In other words, these teachings are the elementary understructure for every Christian. They are as follows:

1. Repentance from acts that lead to death
2. Faith in God
3. Instructions about baptism*s*
4. The laying on of hands
5. The resurrection of the dead
6. Eternal judgment

The Greek word for "elementary" doesn't mean simple, but rather "The initial (starting) point." In other words, these six doctrines come first and are therefore **the *chief* teachings of Christianity**. They're "basic" only in the sense that they're foundational and consequently have priority over other doctrines. As such, this book could also be titled *The SIX CHIEF DOCTRINES of Christianity*.

The more fully you understand these preeminent doctrines the more difficult it will be for anyone to lead you astray with false doctrine. For instance, some Christians falsely teach that it's not necessary for believers to keep in repentance, but the very first elementary doctrine contradicts this. Some say that spiritual rebirth isn't biblical, but the third doctrine disproves this. Many insist that everyone will ultimately be saved regardless of the evil they chose to practice without repentance, but the sixth doctrine refutes this. Simply put, the six basic doctrines will protect you from doctrinal error, including traditional religious doctrines that aren't actually biblical.

Years ago I did a six-part series on these foundational doctrines, one sermon per each teaching. A knowledgeable minister could easily do a series of teachings on every one of them. Unbelievably, in most Christian camps the six basic doctrines are almost utterly ignored. And then ministers wonder why many in their congregations act like spiritual babies. It's because the pastors & teachers aren't properly feeding them! This means, of course, that they're not doing their jobs (Ephesians 4:11-14 & 1 Peter 5:1-4).

The purpose of this book is to **provide foundational structure for younger believers** and, just as importantly, **help more mature believers inspect and fix their foundation as necessary**. Speaking of which…

No believer is in bondage to the doctrinal foundation that was laid in their early years as a Christian. If you come across more accurate biblical data you should adjust your foundation accordingly. I've come across believers who won't change their view on this or that subject because it goes against "how they were taught," no matter how much scriptural evidence is offered to the contrary. This is immaturity where the believer puts the word of some pastor or sect/camp above the Word of God. Please don't be like this. At the same time you shouldn't make changes to your doctrinal foundation at a whim. Don't make any adjustments or repairs until doing a prayerful biblical investigation, like the Bereans did when Paul preached the message of Christ to them (Acts 17:10-12). The truth will set you free (John 8:31-32).

Let's now look at each of the six basic doctrines, one chapter devoted to each. The exception is the sixth doctrine wherein an extra chapter has been added to cover the nature of eternal life. This seventh chapter is essential to our topic and closes the book in a suitably inspiring way.

What's interesting is that the six basic doctrines of Christianity become more involved as you move down the list. As such, the exposition in this book is most detailed concerning the fifth and sixth doctrines, covered in chapters 5, 6 & 7. In other words, the material in *The SIX BASIC DOCTRINES of Christianity* gets more elaborate as we progress.

1

REPENTANCE from Acts that Lead to Death

The word 'repent' simply means to change one's mind for the positive. This doesn't mean a meaningless mental exercise, but a change of mind with the corresponding actions, like the revolve to fulfill God's will (Acts 26:20) and turn from that which is opposed to God's will, meaning sin (Acts 8:22 & 2 Corinthians 12:21). Observe the connection between repentance and faith (belief):

> I have declared to both Jews and Greeks that they must turn to God in <u>repentance</u> <u>and</u> <u>have</u> <u>faith</u> in our Lord Jesus.
>
> **Acts 20:21**

Repentance and faith are two sides of the same coin and so for repentance to be effective it must be combined with faith, which is the second basic doctrine; otherwise repentance is just a dead exercise. Grasping this is vital to spiritual health.

According to Hebrews 6:1 (quoted in the previous chapter), what are we to repent of? "Acts that lead to death." The word 'act' is the same Greek word translated as "act" in this passage:

> **The <u>acts</u> of the flesh are obvious: sexual immorality, impurity and debauchery; [20]idolatry and witchcraft; hatred, discord, jealousy, fits of rage, selfish ambition, dissensions, factions [21] and envy; drunkenness, orgies, and the like. I warn you, as I did before, that those who live like this will not inherit the kingdom of God.**
> **Galatians 5:19-21**

These verses show that "acts of the flesh" aren't limited to just sexual immorality, drunkard-ness, stealing and murder. Things like discord (strife), jealousy, factions (meaning the divisive spirit that results from rigid sectarianism), hatred (aka hostility) and envy are also works of the flesh. Unfortunately, these works are regularly evident in many congregations. Paul warns believers that "those who live like this will not inherit the kingdom of God." In other words, those who practice these sins with no care to repent won't inherit the kingdom of God. This explains why the Bible encourages us to keep 'fessed-up when we miss it:

> **If we claim to be without sin, we deceive ourselves and the truth is not in us. [9] <u>If we confess our sins</u>, he is faithful and just and will forgive us our sins and purify us from all unrighteousness.**
> **1 John 1:8-9**

When we miss it we need to be quick to repent. This takes humility, of course, but humility is good because God's favor flows to the humble, not the proud. In fact, the LORD *resists* or *opposes* the proud, which is why He doesn't offer forgiveness to the unrepentant (James 4:6 & 1 Peter 5:5). This explains Christ's declaration: "But unless you repent you will all perish" (Luke 13:3,5). Arrogant people have an extremely hard time admitting when they're wrong, which is why they won't repent. By contrast, humble folk will readily confess when they miss it; and it's humility that unlocks God's favor.

"Keeping with Repentance"

Observe how John the Baptist referred to regularly confessing sin:

> **"Produce fruit in keeping with repentance."**
> **Matthew & Luke 3:8**

The repentance/forgiveness dynamic is fundamental to your walk with the Lord because it enables you to **1.** get back up when you inevitably miss it, **2.** receive God's forgiveness, **3.** have your slate wiped clean, and **4.** continue to progress forward. It's difficult to bear fruit unto God while knowingly walking in unrepentant sin, to say the least. The principle of "keeping with repentance" assures the continuing stream of the LORD's forgiveness and favor in our lives as we faithfully 'fess up (1 John 1:5-9). Needless to say, don't allow unconfessed sin to block-up your spiritual arteries from the flow of God's grace.

Humbly 'fessing-up should become a regular activity in the life of the believer (Proverbs 28:13 & Psalm 32:5). It's particularly helpful for believers who are in bondage to a certain sin. They want free, but they keep falling back into the sin in question and confessing. This keeping-with-repentance principle ensures the flow of the LORD's forgiveness and favor into their lives. As they seek the Lord and continue in God's Word they will eventually walk in freedom. I was once one of these people, but no longer struggle with any certain sin, which is different than saying I never miss it. A couple days ago I missed it and felt so convicted; I immediately confessed and received the Lord's grace. Praise God!

Repentance from Dead Works

While it's clear that the first basic doctrine refers to repenting of works of the flesh, the terminology in the Greek is open enough to interpret it as "repentance from dead works," which is how the King James Version and English Standard Version put it. As such, the first basic doctrine includes repenting from dead religious works performed to obtain reconciliation with God and eternal salvation. This, by the way, is the definition of human-made religion, which Christ said doesn't work. Notice what the Lord said to the disciples when they asked who could be saved:

> **"With people it is impossible, but not with God;
> for all things are possible with God."**
> **Mark 10:27**

Eternal salvation and everything that goes with it—reconciliation with the LORD, forgiveness of sins and the acquisition of eternal life—are only available through God and not human religion, including religious "Christianity," which isn't actual Christianity. These awesome blessings are available exclusively from God through the gospel, which explains why 'gospel' literally means "good news."

Summary

The first doctrine of Christianity is to repent of—and keep in repentance of—acts of the sinful nature and dead religious works. This is why the gospel is referred to as "repentance **unto life**" in the Bible (Acts 11:18).

We'll look at repentance more, but first let's consider the second basic doctrine of Christianity…

2

FAITH in God

Faith in God is the second basic doctrine because, as the Bible says:

> And <u>without faith it is impossible to please God</u>, because anyone who comes to him <u>must</u> <u>believe</u> that he exists and that he rewards those who earnestly seek him.
> **Hebrews 11:6**

Faith is vital because it's impossible to please God without it. What exactly is faith?

Faith is belief, but not in the sense of believing in fairy tales or casual mental assent. It's belief based on **1.** what is intrinsically obvious, **2.** accurate knowledge, whether scientific, spiritual or otherwise, **3.** genuine revelation by the Holy Spirit, or **4.** some combination of these three.

Let's consider examples of the first three. Regarding #1, someone may say they believe in the concept of God as Creator because it's obvious that the earth, universe and all living creatures were intelligently designed. Or someone may believe homosexuality is intrinsically wrong because the design and function of the sexual organs is obvious (tab 'A' fits into slot 'B'). In each case the person believes based on what is clearly evidence. Concerning #2, people may believe they have a brain even though they've never seen it because medical science has proven it through dissecting human remains, brain surgery, etc. So the person believes based on sound data. Regarding #3, some may turn to God because the Holy Spirit revealed reality to them and they believed it. Their belief is based on the enlightenment of the Holy Spirit.

The Bible calls faith **the substance of things hoped for** and being certain of what we do not see (Hebrews 11:1). The Amplified Bible amplifies the original Greek text thusly:

> **Now faith is the assurance (the confirmation, the title deed) of the things [we] hope for, being the proof of things [we] do not see and the conviction of their reality [faith perceiving as real fact what is not revealed to the senses].**
> **Hebrews 11:1** (Amplified)

Faith is the "title deed" of the things we hope for; that is, the things we righteously desire. In short, **faith is the substance that brings the world of hope or desire into reality!** In the Gospels, for instance, people would come to Jesus hoping for healing and after receiving it the Lord would say something like "Your faith has healed you" (see, for example, Mark 5:25-34). You see? Faith was the substance that brought them what they hoped for—healing. They were certain—convinced—that Christ would heal them even though they couldn't yet see it physically.

Faith for Salvation & Eternal Life

All of this reveals why faith is necessary to receive God's gracious gift of reconciliation and eternal life. After all, how can someone receive a gift from someone he/she doesn't even believes exists? For example, if you said you had a gift for me and I responded by saying I can't receive it because I don't believe you exist, would you still force the gift on me? Of course not. More likely, you'd be irked at my stupidity and arrogance. The same principle applies to those who reject the gospel. When you come across people who do this, be sure to pray that the LORD open their eyes to the truth, i.e. reality.

Did you ever wonder why faith is so important to receiving salvation? Because **faith is nothing more or less than believing God**. That's precisely what Adam & Eve failed to do when they were tested in the Garden of Eden and that's why they fell (see Genesis 2:15-3:24). In other words, **the fall of humanity came about due to unbelief and therefore humanity's restoration is dependent upon belief**.

Everyone has Faith, but Not Necessarily Faith in God

In a sense, every human soul has faith, which explains why we're incurably religious as a species (even those who claim to not believe in God develop belief systems and institutions that have all the earmarks of what is generally perceived as "religion"[1]).

---

[1] For instance, secular humanism—essentially one-in-the-same as far Left "liberalism"—has its own cosmology, its own miracles, its own beliefs in the supernatural, its own "churches" (public schools & secular universities), its own "high priests" (godless professors and teachers), its own "saints" (thugs), its own worldview and its own explanation of the existence of the universe. While

Belief in God is simply a part of our make-up; it's in our spiritual DNA. Heck, creation itself inspires belief in God; more than that, creation screams out God's existence (Psalm 19:1-4 & Romans 1:18-20). To suggest that everything in the universe came about through accident and that there's no Intelligent Designer is like expecting a Boeing 747 to emerge out of a metal scrapyard after millions of years. It's absurd.

Unfortunately, as Paul put it, unbelievers "are darkened in their understanding and separated from the life of God because of the ignorance that is in them due to the hardening of their hearts" (Ephesians 4:18). In other words, they have faith but they've willingly hardened their hearts to it, consciously or subconsciously. Why? For a number of reasons, such as not wanting to give up some pet sin or lifestyle, but often simply because that's how their godless culture brainwashed them and they choose to run with the pack. So they deny obvious reality.

Hardening their hearts to their intrinsic faith in God, they redirect their faith to something else, like a godless government party and the smooth politicians thereof, e.g. the Demonic-rats. Or the idea that humans originated from apes even though there's zero evidence of a "missing link." And so on.

Repentance and Faith

It's interesting that repentance and faith are the first two basic doctrines of Christianity because these are the *conditions* to receiving God's gift of eternal salvation:

---

this is generally true, it shouldn't be interpreted to mean that *all* professors, public school teachers, scientists, judges, etc. are **LIE**beral secular humanists because this isn't true in the least.

> **I have declared to both Jews and Greeks that they must turn to God <u>in repentance</u> and <u>have faith</u> in our Lord Jesus.**
>
> **Acts 20:21**

We effectively "turn to God" via the gospel through **repentance** and **faith**. This was made clear in Christ's first sermon upon entering public ministry:

> **"The time is fulfilled, and the kingdom of God is at hand; <u>repent</u> and <u>believe</u> in the gospel."**
>
> **Mark 1:15** (ESV)

In the original language "believe" is the verb form of the Greek word for faith. Repentance and faith are the keys to receiving the gospel—the message of Christ—and they are fittingly the first two basic doctrines of Christianity.

'Repentance' inexplicably has a negative connotation in modern times because people misinterpret it to mean that God is trying to prevent them from having a "good time." But sin can only bring a "good time" superficially because underneath the surface pleasure is misery & death for "the wages of sin is death." This is an axiom.

Take, for instance, the "party" lifestyle. When I was a teen I smoked pot, did drugs and drank frequently. It became a lifestyle and it was difficult for me to imagine life without constant "partying." After several years I wisely quit. This was before I even became a believer. In essence, I repented because repentance is simply the resolve to change for the positive and the corresponding action. Why did I quit? Because, although doing these things delivered a quick fix to escape reality and have a "good time," they couldn't deliver the goods in the long term.

Instead they brought hangovers, depression, broken relationships and bondage.

What spurred my change-for-the-positive, i.e. my repentance? I saw the obvious truth, believed it, and changed accordingly. The same principle applies to receiving God's grace of salvation through the gospel of Christ. We see the truth, believe it, and change accordingly. Repentance is the resolve to change for the positive in accordance with reality, which is the truth—the way it really is. Reality is always God's will. And I mean actual reality, not the imaginary realities—or "social constructs"—people dream-up and try to live by, like "gender identity."

To explain, 'truth' is *alétheia (ah-LAY-thee-ah)* in the Greek, meaning reality, **the way it really is** as opposed to the way it really isn't.

Repentance and Faith are Not Works

Repentance and faith are not works, but rather the natural reaction to realizing the truth. "Truth," again, is simply the way it really is. So repentance & faith are **the wise response to seeing the truth, the way it really is**.

Here's an illustration: Say a man sincerely believes that 2 + 2 = 5. This is a false belief whether he *believes* it's true or not. So I go to him with four stones and plainly illustrate that 2 stones plus the other 2 stones equals four stones, not five. He observes the truth—the way it really is—and therefore *believes* and hence *changes his mind*. He now believes that 2 + 2 = 4, which is the truth, the way it really is.

You see? Repentance and faith are not works, but simply the natural response to being exposed to the truth. Only a blind, indoctrinated fool would see the truth—the way it really is—and reject it in favor of his/her incorrect belief.

The New Covenant is a Covenant of FAITH

Our covenant with God is a covenant of faith and so everything in our covenant is by faith. Covenant means contract or agreement. Do you want eternal salvation? It's by faith. Healing? It's by faith. Intimacy with God? Faith. Answers to prayer? Faith. Power to overcome? Faith.

In light of this I find it perplexing when I come across Christians who are "anti-faith" because it's a total oxymoron. They defend their position on the grounds that there have been some extremists in the faith movement, but every movement in the body of Christ inspired by the Holy Spirit has its lunatic fringe. You don't throw the baby out with the bathwater!

Faith *and* Perseverance (Patience)

One thing about faith needs to be stressed: Faith must be combined with perseverance—patient endurance—or what you're hoping for will not come to pass. This is why the Bible says:

> **We do not want you to become lazy, but to imitate those who through faith <u>and patience</u> inherit what has been promised.**
>
> **Hebrews 6:12**

This is just common sense. After all, **faith isn't really faith if you give up**. It might be temporary, fleeting faith, but it's not the faith that can withstand the time of testing, which includes *the wait* before the manifestation (Luke 8:13). Even salvation can be lost if one doesn't persevere in the faith, as shown in this passage:

> **Once you were alienated from God and were enemies in your minds because of your evil behavior. ^{22} But now he has reconciled you by Christ's physical body through death to present you holy in his sight, without blemish and free from accusation—^{23} <u>if you continue in your faith</u>, established and firm, and do not move from the hope held out in the gospel.**
> **Colossians 1:21-23**

We have eternal security in Christ. The Lord said so and it's 100% true (John 10:27-30). But eternal security is not the same as *unconditional* eternal security because reconciliation with God and eternal life are **the result of faith** in the message of Christ, the gospel. In other words, if it takes faith to be saved, a person who doesn't persevere and thus gives up on faith is no longer saved. I'm not talking about someone experiencing doubts, but rather giving up on faith in Christ altogether. It's the difference between stumbling and utterly falling away in outright rebellion (Hebrews 6:4-9). *All* believers struggle & stumble at times in their spiritual journey, especially when we're immature; only faithless rebels fall away.

Faith *IN* GOD

Someone might argue that the second basic doctrine of Christianity is technically "faith **in God**" (Hebrews 6:1-2) and therefore only refers to believing the LORD personally. Yes, it refers to believing the LORD personally, but faith in God also includes believing whatever the LORD has created that testifies to God's existence or will.

For instance, all creation is a physical testimony to the existence of the Almighty and therefore inspires faith (belief) in the Creator. One of the reasons I was an agnostic and not a strict atheist before I accepted the message of Christ is because the earth & universe and all living things cried out that there was an Intelligent Designer (Psalm 19:1-4 & Romans 1:18-20). I simply wasn't stupid enough to be an atheist, keeping in mind that true atheists stubbornly say they *know* there is no Creator with almost zero doubt. This shows, by the way, that they have faith, just not faith in God.

Consider also the testimony of God's amazing Word: The Lord *is* truth and His Word *is* truth and therefore His Word testifies to His existence (John 14:6 & 17:17).

Faith in God, not Faith in Faith

The doctrine of faith in God shows that our faith is the result of knowing the LORD—which means the result of relationship—as well as knowing God's word & promises. So it's faith in God, not faith in faith.

In other words, the power in biblical faith stems from its object—God. Genuine faith must have an object and that object is the character of the Almighty Creator. It's not something in our flesh that makes faith work, but rather the character of God combined with the faith that spring from our human spirit, as well as the indwelling Holy Spirit (Proverbs 20:27, Titus 3:5 & 1 Corinthians 6:19). Faith—belief—is simply the natural response to God, God's Word and God's creation. This prevents faith from becoming a human work and gives all the glory of our faith exploits to the LORD.

Needless to say, this is an encouragement to go deeper in your relationship with the Lord and to grow in the knowledge of God's Word and the promises thereof (2 Peter 3:18), as well as the promises the Holy Spirit gives to you personally.

How Does Faith Grow?

The starting point for every believer is faith because our covenant with God is a covenant of faith. 'Covenant' means "an agreement or pact having terms determined by the initiating party, which are also affirmed by the one entering the agreement." A good English word for covenant is contract. All Christians have a contract with Father God through Christ by the Holy Spirit. This is the New *Covenant* or New *Testament*. Everything we receive in our agreement with the LORD is by faith because "without faith it is impossible to please God, because anyone who comes to him must believe that he exists and that he rewards those who earnestly seek him" (Hebrews 11:6).

The Bible says that every believer has a "measure of faith" otherwise they wouldn't be a believer (Romans 12:3). It's a done deal—"God has distributed" the measure of faith to everyone who's a believer. It's a gift from God (Ephesians 2:8-9) and every believer starts with the same measure.

However, it's clear that faith can grow. For instance, Jesus noted the "little faith" of his disciples on occasion (Luke 12:28 & Matthew 14:28–31), which shows that they *could* have had more faith. In 2 Thessalonians 1:3 Paul observed that the faith of the Thessalonian believers was "growing more and more" and in 2

Corinthians 10:15 he clearly expected the Corinthians' faith to "continue to grow." Your faith can likewise increase, but it's dependent on YOU adding the seven qualities relayed in 2 Peter 1:5-7—goodness, knowledge, self-control (i.e. practicing the knowledge you acquire), perseverance, godliness, mutual (Christian) affection and love.

You'll note that there are seven virtues. This is fitting since the number 7 is identified with something being "finished" or "complete" in the Bible. Thus, if you are diligent to add these seven qualities to your walk you will be complete as a man or woman of God. Praise the Lord! You can read more about how to add these seven qualities to your faith at the Fountain of Life site; see the article *The Seven Keys to SPIRITUAL GROWTH*.[2]

---

[2] Also available in chapters 7 & 8 of my book *The Four Stages of Spiritual Growth*.

3

Instructions about BAPTISMS

The third basic doctrine is biblical instructions about baptisms. The Greek word for 'baptize' is *baptizó (bap-TID-zoh)*, which means "overwhelmed, covered or submerged." It was used in reference to being "baptized" by debts in ancient times. The noun form is in the plural in Hebrews 6:2 because **there are three baptisms in Christianity**. Most Christians only know about water baptism, which ironically is the least important (which is different than saying it's unimportant). Every believer should experience all three baptisms, but it's the first one that *must* be experienced in order to be a Christian. The three baptisms are:

1. Baptism into Christ
2. Water baptism.
3. The baptism of the Holy Spirit.

Let's address all three:

Baptism into Christ

This refers to being spiritually born-again through Christ. Notice what the Scriptures say about this baptism:

> **So in Christ Jesus you are all children of God through faith, ²⁷ for all of you who were <u>baptized into Christ</u> have clothed yourselves with Christ.**
> **Galatians 3:26-27**

> **He saved us, not because of righteous things we had done, but because of his mercy. He saved us through the washing of <u>rebirth and renewal by the Holy Spirit</u>**
> **Titus 3:5**

The obvious reason the baptism into Christ is a foundational doctrine is because it's impossible to be a Christian apart from this new spiritual birth. If someone says they're a believer, but aren't spiritually regenerated then they're a Christian in name only and aren't genuinely saved.

If you come across any minister or group that says people don't have to be spiritually reborn to be a Christian, as Jesus stressed in John 3:3,6, they should be rejected as false teachers. As Christ said about the false teachers of his day: "Leave them; they are blind guides. If the blind lead the blind, both will fall into a pit" (Matthew 15:14).

Water Baptism

Baptism in water is simply **a public testimony of the believer's baptism into Christ**. Acts 10:47-48 is a good example. Here are five things about water baptism you should know:

1. It is an outward expression of a personal decision already made.
2. It symbolizes death to the sin nature.
3. Being lifted out of the water symbolizes resurrection to a new life in Christ (Romans 6:1-4).
4. The water obviously represents the "washing of rebirth and renewal by the Holy Spirit" (Titus 3:5).
5. Believers are to be baptized "in the name of the Father and of the Son and of the Holy Spirit" (Matthew 28:19).

I'm sure you see why water baptism isn't as important as the baptism into Christ since **water baptism is merely the symbolic testimony of what has already taken place spiritually through baptism into Christ**. What's more important, the inward baptism or the outward baptism that represents it?

Baptism of the Holy Spirit

Being baptized into Christ is essentially one-in-the-same as being "born of the Spirit" (John 3:3,6), but being born of the Spirit is distinct from the baptism of the Spirit, although they occasionally happen at the same time. When you're born of the Spirit the Spirit is *in* you (Romans 8:9 & 1 Corinthians 6:19), whereas when you're baptized in the Spirit the Spirit is *all over you* because you're immersed with the Spirit. It's the difference between drinking a glass of water and jumping into a pure, mountain lake.

Speaking in tongues is theoretically the initial physical evidence of the baptism in the Holy Spirit. While speaking in tongues is not the Holy Spirit and the Holy Spirit is not speaking in tongues, they go hand in hand. Here are five scriptural examples of people receiving this baptism:

1. **The believers in Jerusalem, as shown in Acts 2:1-4.** All of them spoke in tongues.
2. **The Samaritans, as shown in Acts 8:12-19.** The Samaritans were part Jew and part Gentile. Verse 18 shows that Simon the sorcerer "saw" that the Spirit was given to the Samaritans when the apostles laid their hands on them. In other words, he saw evidence that they received the Holy Spirit. What did he see? We must interpret Scripture with Scripture, which is a hermeneutical rule. Since the rest of the New Testament shows that speaking in tongues is the initial evidence of the baptism of the Holy Spirit, this must've been what Simon saw—people speaking in languages they didn't know.
3. **Saul in Damascus, as shown in Acts 9:17-18.** Although speaking in tongues is not mentioned in this passage, the baptism of the Holy Spirit is, and we observe scriptural evidence elsewhere that Saul/Paul spoke in tongues on a regular basis, which is praying in the spirit (1 Corinthians 14:18-19).
4. **Cornelius' household in Caesarea, as shown in Acts 10:44-48.** This refers to the first Gentile believers. Verses 45-46 state: "The circumcised believers who had come with Peter were astonished that the gift of the Holy Spirit had been poured out even on the Gentiles. For they heard them speaking in tongues and praising God." Since believers who are not baptized in the spirit can and do praise God, the evidence of the baptism is obviously speaking in tongues.
5. **The Ephesians, as shown in Acts 19:5-7.** This passage shows that all twelve spoke in tongues as a result of receiving the baptism, not just a select few.

As already noted every Christian can and should receive this baptism and pray in the spirit to supplement prayer in his or her native language. This can be observed in 1 Corinthians 14:14-15, 18-19 and Ephesians 6:18. I have to emphasize this because there's this idea rampant in the body of Christ that speaking in tongues was done away with once the biblical canon was completed, which is known as cessationism. Don't believe it. It's a colossal lie that has allowed the enemy to keep multitudes of sincere believers from the full empowerment and help of the Holy Spirit.

Praying in the spirit is important because it edifies us by building us up in faith and empowers us to minister, to love people and to walk free from sin.

Before we get into that, there are a few things about the baptism of the Spirit and speaking in tongues that need to be stressed and clarified:

- Just because a Christian is baptized in the Spirit and can speak in tongues, it does not mean that he or she is walking in the spirit and producing the fruit thereof, like love, joy, peace, kindness, faith, humility and self-control (Galatians 5:22-23). Putting it another way, to be spirit-controlled is synonymous with bearing fruit of the spirit but just because a believer is baptized in the Spirit and can speak in tongues it does not mean that he or she is participating in the divine nature, that is, walking in the spirit and producing the fruit thereof (Galatians 5:16).
- With the above understanding, the baptism of the Holy Spirit and the corresponding gift of glossolalia should not be taken as a badge of superiority where the believer becomes condescending toward those who don't (yet) have it. To do this would be arrogance and "God opposes the proud." Spirit-baptized believers who cop a pompous attitude will naturally slip into legalism. Speaking of which,

there are plenty of tongues-talking legalists in the body of Christ—too many!
- Although the baptism of the Holy Spirit is wonderful and empowering—which is why the Bible stresses it—it should not be viewed as a "cure all" or the all-and-end-all of Christianity.
- If a Christian can walk in the spirit to a good degree without the baptism of the Holy Spirit, how much more so if they are baptized in the Holy Spirit? In other words, just because you're doing well spiritually without speaking in tongues, don't let it rob you of this wonderful gift that God has provided for all believers!
- The baptism of the Holy Spirit is usually transferred through physical contact, that is, via the ministry of laying on of hands, but not always. While the gift can be received through someone who already has it, as shown in some of the above examples, a believer can also receive it simply through faith without a human conduit (Luke 11:9-13). In fact, everything in our covenant is by faith.
- If any believer has hands laid on him or her for this baptism and they don't speak in tongues it doesn't necessarily mean they didn't receive the baptism. They may have received it, but simply have yet to speak in tongues. We have to understand that speaking in tongues—praying in the spirit—is something that the believer does by his or her volition and is not something the Holy Spirit makes people do. Remember what Paul said: "So what shall *I* do? *I* will pray with my spirit, but *I* will also pray with my mind" (1 Corinthians 14:15). Just as praying in a language you understand is an act of your own will, so is praying in the spirit. With this understanding, if I so chose I could theoretically not pray in the spirit the rest of my life even though I am baptized in the Spirit. Are you following?

- On that note, there are too many Christians who are baptized in the Spirit and yet rarely, if ever, pray in the spirit. They therefore lack the empowerment the Holy Spirit wants to give them. Speaking of which…

The Empowerment and Help of the Holy Spirit

The baptism of the Spirit and corresponding praying in the spirit are God-given sources of great empowerment for the believer to walk in newness of life and victory. Unfortunately, many believers settle for less than God's best and so they go through life struggling with things they don't have to struggle with because God has provided the power and help they need—if only they knew of these truths and implemented them! It is for this purpose that God detailed these truths in his Word and it's why I'm stressing them here.

Notice the power that Paul said was available for his protégé Timothy:

> **For this reason I remind you to fan into flame the gift of God, which is in you through the laying on of hands. ⁷ For God did not give us a spirit of timidity, but a spirit of <u>power</u>, of <u>love</u> and of <u>self-discipline</u>.**
> **2 Timothy 1:6-7**

What gift was Paul talking about? He doesn't say, but there are clues: The gift was given through the laying on of hands and it is linked to the spirit or Spirit. Since Scripture interprets Scripture we must conclude that Paul was referring to the baptism of the Holy Spirit because **1.** this gift involves the Spirit, **2.** there's repeated evidence that this gift is typically transferred through the laying on of hands, as detailed in the previous section, and **3.** this gift involves Spirit-given power. The baptism of the Spirit is the obvious answer.

By instructing Timothy to "fan into flame" this gift, Paul was simply encouraging Timothy to pray in the spirit more often, which is actually the seventh piece of the armor of God (Ephesians 6:18). What does he mean by fanning it into flame? Speaking from experience, when I first received the baptism of the Holy Spirit in 1986—two and a half years after my salvation—I'd generally keep saying the same phrase over and over in the spirit. It was just a handful of words and I had no idea what I was saying. Regardless, I put into practice this passage: I fanned the gift into flame by praying in the spirit whenever I had the opportunity, like driving to classes or to work or when I went off by myself to pray (Luke 5:16). In time my spiritual prayer language grew dramatically. How so? Because I fanned it into flame just as Paul instructed Timothy. This is the key to walking in the three blessings cited in verse 7: **power, love** and **self-discipline**. Let's take a look at each of these…

Power

One of the main purposes of the baptism of the Holy Spirit is for believers to be empowered to walk in newness of life and be witnesses to the world (Luke 24:49 & Acts 1:8). The Greek word for power is *dunamis (DOO-nah-miss)*, which is where we get the English words dynamo and dynamite. 'Dynamo' bespeaks of electrical power or a really energetic, forceful person, and 'dynamite' suggests explosive power. These are earthly things. Imagine how much greater is God's dunamis power that's available to all believers through the baptism of the Holy Spirit! All we have to do is fan it into flame and *keep it* flaming.

When Paul said, "Do not get drunk on wine, which leads to debauchery. Instead, be filled with the Spirit" (Ephesians 5:18) he meant it in the sense of *keep being* filled. In other words, praying in the spirit is an ongoing thing. Why do you think Jude said: "But you, dear friends, build yourselves up in your most holy faith and pray in the Holy Spirit" (Jude 1:20)? Why do you think Paul instructed: "And pray in the Spirit on all occasions with all kinds of prayers and requests" (Ephesians 6:18)? It should be an ongoing activity. We don't pray in the spirit and then never do it again; that would be absurd. It's a *daily* thing.

If you have the baptism of the Holy Spirit, I encourage you to pray in the spirit as soon as you get out of bed in the morning and as loud as possible; sing in the spirit as well, as Paul exemplified (1 Corinthians 14:14-15). Singing in the spirit, by the way, is merely praying in the spirit to a melody, like you're singing a song. Paul practiced this and he was a powerhouse for God, second only to Jesus Christ himself in the New Testament. If you want to be a powerhouse like him you'll have to do what he did. He's our biblical example.

You can pray in the spirit or sing in the spirit while you're making coffee or taking a shower or driving. How long you do this is between you and God (try 5-10 minutes), just do it and keep doing it—charge yourself up every morning and throughout the day. It's more powerful than strong coffee. In a sense, it's the ultimate drug because it's free and you don't have to deal with hangovers, not to mention the supply never runs out.

Think again about dunamis power—dynamite power. Does this sound like a boring thing? A deathly religious thing? No, it suggests the abundant life that the Messiah said he came to give us:

> **The thief comes only to steal and kill and destroy; I have come that they may have <u>life</u> and <u>have it to the full</u>.**
>
> John 10:10

The very reason Jesus came was to give us life and life to the full! When you get around Christians infected by legalism the last thing you'll discern is life-to-the-full and all that comes with it—joy, excitement, energy, ideas, faith, strength, confidence, love, creativity, originality, etc. More likely you'll witness a stuffy, dead, dull, powerless, hackneyed religious spirit. It's a horrible shame. This is the image secular culture has of Christians, but it's a false image and, thankfully, we don't have to be like that. Praise God!

Do you want dynamite power at work in your life every day? Then pray in the spirit more and more! This is the very reason the LORD gave us the gift of speaking in tongues, not to argue with non-Charismatics!

Love

The type of love we're empowered to walk in by praying in the spirit is agape love, which is purely practical love or love-in-action; this type of love isn't dependent on affinity or affection. It's important to distinguish this because there are four types of love observed in the Bible:

1. Storge love is family love, which includes the bond, affection and loyalty that develops between family members. Although the word itself, *storge (STOR-gay)*, is not found in the original text we see numerous examples of this type of love in the Bible, like Martha & Mary's love for their brother Lazarus in John 11.

Of course, the opposite of storge love can develop between family members, which is when relatives develop hatred for each other. A couple of obvious examples are Cain & Abel (Genesis 4:1-11) and Joseph & his jealous brothers (Genesis 37).

2. Phileo love is friendship love or brotherly love, like the platonic affection/respect of David and Jonathan (2 Samuel 1:25-26). Philadelphia, "the city of brotherly love," was named after this type of love. You could say that phileo love is storge love applied to non-family members. There's an element of affection, respect or bond despite the fact that they're not kin. The word *phileo (fil-LAY-oh)* can be found some 25 times in the original Greek text of the New Testament whereas the noun form, *philia (fil-EE-ah)*, appears only once (which is why we're using phileo here and not philia).

Jesus' phileo love for Martha, Mary and Lazarus is a good example of this form of love, as observed here:

> [5] **Now Jesus <u>loved</u> *(phileo)* Martha and her sister and Lazarus...**
> [35] **Jesus wept.**
> [36] **Then the Jews said, "See how he <u>loved</u> *(phileo)* him!"**
>
> **John 11:5, 35-36**

3. Eros love is phileo love between members of the opposite sex and includes a romantic element, but it doesn't refer to shallow sexual lust. Although the word *eros (eer-ROSS)* doesn't appear in the original manuscripts there are many examples of this type of love in the Scriptures. One overt example can be observed in the amazing Song of Songs. Here's a passionate expression of love from this book where the man is speaking to the woman:

> show me your face,
>> let me hear your voice;
> for your voice is sweet,
>> and your face is lovely.
>
> Song of Songs 2:14

4. Agape love is, again, purely practical love or love-in-action and is therefore not dependent on liking/respecting a person. It's usually described as divine love, which is true since "God is love," but it's really just practical love or love-in-practice regardless of bond/respect/affection. In other words, you can agape love someone for whom you have zero kinship (storge love), esteem/rapport (phileo love) or romantic fondness (eros love). Note the biblical definition:

> **Love** *(agape)* **is patient, love is kind. It does not envy. It does not boast, it is not proud. [5] It is not rude, it is not self-seeking, it is not easily angered, it keeps no record of wrongs. [6] Love does not delight in evil but rejoices with the truth. [7] It always protects, always trusts, always hopes, always perseveres.**
>
> 1 Corinthians 13:4-7

Paul gave this definition of agape love by the Holy Spirit to encourage believers to practice agape love. Notice that he doesn't say anything about having warm feelings or respect toward the other person when applying agape love. Why? Because agape love refers purely to practical love, which is distinguished from storge love (familial love), phileo love (friendship love) and eros love (romantic love), each of which involve some type of connection, closeness or warm feelings. It's easy to walk in love toward people for whom you have kinship, respect or affection, but it's not so easy when you don't.

Think about it like this: The most famous passage of Scripture says "God so loved *(agape)* the world that he gave his one and only Son, that whoever believes in him shall not perish but have eternal life." Do you think this means that God has warm, fuzzy feelings for all the tyrants, warmongers, abusers, God-haters, rapists, murderers, molesters and perverts out there? Do you think he's up there with dreamy eyes saying, "Oh, I just so respect and love these wicked people!" Of course not. The passage is referring to agape love—purely practical love. The Father was *practicing* love when he had his one and only Son die for our sins; the Son did the same when he willingly laid down his life. This opened the door for reconciliation and eternal life for fallen humanity through spiritual rebirth. God made the first move, humanity didn't. The question is, how are we going to respond to his incredible example of agape love?

Those who respond positively to God's agape love and accept the gospel immediately enter into his storge love since they are born into God's family (1 John 3:9). These are candidates for becoming the Lord's friend, which has to do with phileo love and the favor that comes with it. As noted, phileo love refers to friendship love or brotherly love. Consider Jesus' statement to his disciples:

"You are my friends if you do what I command."
John 15:14

According to this verse not everyone is Jesus' friend, not even every believer, who is part of God's family and therefore possesses his storge love. Christ's friends are limited to those who practice what he commands. This refers to believers who respect the Lord enough to know Him & His Word and put it into practice, as well as obey the directions of the Spirit. God's grace (favor) for salvation is for all and is unmerited; it is simply received through humble repentance and faith (Acts 20:21), but this doesn't mean we can't increase in favor with God after we receive salvation. Why do you think the Scriptures say that Jesus—who is our example—grew in favor with God just as he grew in favor with people (Luke 2:52)? Why do you think Peter encouraged us to grow in the grace (favor) of our Lord and Savior Jesus Christ, just as we are to grow in knowledge (2 Peter 3:18)?

Sad to say, these simple truths are blasphemy in some circles of Christianity. It's both ignorant and shameful.

My point is that agape love is purely practical in nature and therefore you don't have to feel any warmth or respect toward the person or people with whom you share it. In short, agape is love-in-action and has little to do with affection, that is, liking the person. This explains how we can fulfill Jesus & Paul's instructions to love our enemies (Luke 6:27 & Romans 12:20-21). Do you like your enemies, that is, phileo love them? Do you respect them? Of course you don't. But this isn't a problem because we are not commanded to phileo love our enemies, but rather to agape love them. Are you following?

This shows why agape love is often defined as "unconditional love" since it is purely practical in nature and, again, not dependent upon liking an individual or on how well they treat you. Here's an example: I was at my desk in my den and had a few greeting cards ready to mail out on the side of my desk. Carol came in and noticed that one of the cards was made out to someone who's been known to treat us—particularly me—with contempt and slander. She said, "Oh, what a warmhearted soul you are." Actually, it wasn't a big deal because I'm empowered by the spirit to love those who hate me without cause. It's been my regular practice for years. My flesh may not want to do it, but I strive to be spirit-controlled and not flesh-ruled. The main reason some believers have difficulty in doing this is because **1.** they're not walking in the spirit and therefore not producing the fruit thereof, the primary fruit being agape love (Galatians 5:19-23), **2.** they're not baptized in the Spirit or **3.** if they are, they're not praying in the spirit because praying in the spirit charges the believer up and empowers us to agape love our enemies and "overcome evil with good" (Romans 12:20-21).

By the way, when I refer to walking in love, I'm not referring to just the gentle variety. There's something called *tough* love since agape love "is kind" and "does not delight in evil." Sometimes the kindest thing you can do for people is to boldly confront the evil that has infected them, like Paul when he openly rebuked Peter for his legalism (Galatians 2:11-14) and Christ when he radically cleared the temple while yelling, pushing over tables and cracking a whip (Mark 11:15-18 & John 2:13-16). Some Christians think they're walking in agape love by being nicey-wicey doormats when, in fact, they're being cowardly and enabling evil to persist. I should hastily add that this isn't an excuse to be a rash fool who's overly gung-ho with confronting and rebuking, which is abusive and usually results in unnecessary strife.

Needless to say, if you want a more effective love walk, keep yourself filled with the Spirit by praying in the spirit and fanning into flame the agape love that's necessary to practice it.

Self-control

I've been in the Lord since 1984 and I've overcome certain struggles of the flesh as I've grown spiritually and continue to do so, but I know believers from the 1980s and 90s who are still struggling with the very same issues they had back then. I'm talking about things like alcoholism, drugs, depression, porn addiction and government idolatry. They never attained the self-control necessary to walk in victory in these areas. I don't mean fleshly self-control here, but rather the Spirit-empowered discipline necessary to strip off such bondages and walk according to the spirit, which naturally produces the fruit of the spirit, one of which is self-control.

If a believer is walking in spiritual self-control they'll have the power and discipline to walk free of fleshly bondages. This is something that develops over time, but praying in the spirit is key to producing this dunamis power and the necessary discipline, not to mention the other two keys to walking in the Spirit.

Notice what Jesus said about the purpose of the baptism of the Holy Spirit:

> [5] **"but in a few days you will be baptized with the Holy Spirit..."**
> [8] **"But you will receive power when the Holy Spirit comes on you; and you will be my witnesses in Jerusalem, and in all Judea and Samaria, and to the ends of the earth."**
> **Acts 1:5,8**

The purpose of the baptism of the Holy Spirit is to empower believers. Empowering believers to be witnesses means more than just the oomph it takes to share the gospel with people verbally, it includes the power to walk free of the flesh, including legalism and libertinism. After all, how effective is a witness who lacks the power to walk free of the bondages of the flesh?

The Messiah also said this about the Holy Spirit:

> "But the Counselor, the Holy Spirit, whom the Father will send in my name, will teach you all things and will remind you of everything I have said to you."
>
> **John 14:26**

Here Christ describes the Holy Spirit as our "Counselor," which is translated as "Helper" in the King James Version. He goes on to say that the Counselor will teach us all things. Yeshua described this as guiding us "into all truth" in John 16:13. Needless to say, if you want more understanding and insight to the Scriptures and the will of God, pray in the spirit more often.

As far as the Spirit being our helper, Paul said this:

> In the same way, the Spirit helps us in our weakness. We do not know what we ought to pray for, but the Spirit himself intercedes for us with groans that words cannot express.
>
> **Romans 8:26**

One of the purposes of the Holy Spirit—our "Helper"—is to help us in our weaknesses. The Spirit does this by interceding for us, which takes place when we pray in the spirit. When we speak in tongues the Holy Ghost guides our spirit what to pray and, hence, intercedes for us. This can include "groans that words cannot express," which I've experienced on some occasions while praying in the spirit (Romans 8:26).

What we want to focus on here is that the Holy Spirit is our Helper who helps us in our weaknesses. As shared above, I've known believers who have problems in areas like alcohol, drugs, depression, porn addiction, one form of sexual immorality or another, lying and gossip/slander. In other words, they're weak in these areas. The good news is that one of the very purposes of the Holy Spirit is to empower believers to overcome in such areas, but we have to be baptized in the Spirit and fan into flame the gift—praying in the spirit on all occasions. As we do this, we'll cultivate the power from within to overcome in any area of weakness. This is spiritual power, not fleshly power. Let me give an example from my own life.

I used to have a huge problem with depression. Two professional Christian counselors said I needed to be on medication, but I knew that wasn't the route to go. If other believers choose to go on medication for a season, that's between them and the LORD, but—for me—it wasn't the way to go. I just knew it. So I kept following the Lord and growing in the Spirit. After a while, I noticed that the Spirit would lead my spirit to sometimes laugh uproariously while praying in the spirit. For example, there are times when I'm tempted to get blue, but instead I pray in the spirit and my spirit inspires me to laugh like crazy as led of the Holy Spirit. This has nothing to do with my mental state since laughing is the farthest thing from my mind on these occasions, but as my spirit prompts me to laugh uproariously with knee-slapping laughter I am naturally influenced by it—it rubs off. Needless to say, it keeps me out of depression! You see: The Holy Spirit helps me in my area of weakness and enables me to overcome.

If you have an area of weakness—and who doesn't?—charge yourself up regularly by praying in the spirit and the Holy Spirit will give you the power to overcome and walk in victory, I guarantee it. It may not happen overnight, but it *will* happen and one day you'll look back at your current struggle and laugh. Your weakness will come to mind and you'll just laugh about it!

Your weakness may not even be something of the flesh but simply a trait that's unique to you. For instance, you might have an extreme loathing for the punch-the-clock grind. The Holy Spirit will help you in this area of "weakness" as well. He'll give ideas, golden connections or open doors for you to make a living without the drudgery of punching a clock. Whatever your weakness or need is, the Holy Spirit is here and he's *in* you to *help* you!

4

The Laying on of Hands

The doctrine of the laying on of hands refers to the transference of four things through physical contact: **1.** blessing, **2.** anointing and consecration for service, that is, ministry, **3.** the baptism of the Holy Spirit, and **4.** healing and deliverance.

Let's look at all four...

Blessing (or General Prayer)

Jesus placed his hands on children and blessed them (Mark 10:13,16 & Matthew 19:13,15). To 'bless' someone means to speak positive words that have a productive impact. The official priestly prayer supports this definition (Numbers 6:22-27) and you can find these types of prayer/blessings all over the Bible, e.g. Romans 15:13 and Colossians 1:9-12.

Blessing or prayer in this manner is so important because words "have the power of life and death" (Proverbs 18:21). Whether people know it or not, our words bring either life or death, blessing or cursing. Proverbs 12:18 reinforces this: "Reckless words pierce like a sword, but the tongue of the wise brings healing."

Needless to say, the idea that "words can never hurt me" is a lie.

Kids and youth are especially vulnerable to "reckless words" or verbal abuse, particularly from authority figures in their lives (Colossians 3:21). Adults who continually berate, belittle and call children names are speaking a prophecy of death and destruction over them (!).

Blessing, by contrast, is a prophecy of life, which is why Jesus laid his hands on children and blessed them.

Words are powerful by themselves; adding the dimension of touch magnifies their impact.

Anointing/Separation for Ministry

Hands are to be lain on those called of God to special service. Biblical examples include the Levites (Numbers 8:10-11), Joshua, (Numbers 27:18-23), Stephen & six others (Acts 6:1-6) and Saul & Barnabas (Acts 13:2-3).

Obviously the people who qualify for such a rite of passage should already be full of faith, God's Word and the Spirit, as was the case with Joshua and Steven in the examples cited. The laying on of hands simply provides a stronger anointing to fulfill their God-given assignment.

Paul instructed his young protégé, Timothy, to not be "hasty in the laying on of hands" (1 Timothy 5:22) because ministers must be tested for character and faithfulness and there's no test like the test of time. Those who hastily confirm untested ministers share responsibility for the damage they eventually do to people.

The Holy Spirit Baptism

Hands are to be laid on believers to receive the baptism of the Holy Spirit, which is evidenced by speaking in tongues (Acts 19:1-7).

While this powerful gift is typically received this way—that is, through someone who has it—a believer can also receive it simply through faith in God's Word (Luke 11:9-13). In other words, believers don't absolutely need a human conduit for the gift to be transferred. We'll look at this concept more in the next section.

For details on the Holy Spirit baptism and glossolalia see the sections in the previous chapter: *Baptism of the Holy Spirit* and *The Empowerment and Help of the Holy Spirit*.

Healing and Spiritual Deliverance

Jesus prophesied that believers "will place their hands on sick people, and they will get well" (Mark 16:17-18).

The book of Acts says "God anointed Jesus of Nazareth with the Holy Spirit and power, and… he went around doing good and healing all who were under the power of the devil, because God was with him" (Acts 10:38). We see evidence of this throughout the Gospels. Here are some examples plus vital additional info:

- Jesus laid hands on sick people and healed them or exorcized demons from them (Luke 4:40-41).

- A woman who was subject to bleeding for twelve years heard about Jesus' anointing to heal and therefore had faith to receive healing from him (Mark 5:25-34). When the woman touched his cloak Christ sensed "power had gone out from him" (verse 30).
- The Messiah had an anointing to heal, but his ministry was very limited in his hometown because of the people's lack of faith due to a "spirit of familiarity"—meaning they were so familiar with Jesus during his first three decades that they were hindered from acknowledging his divine anointing and receiving from it (Mark 6:1-6). This example reveals that getting a healing is a matter of faith in regards to **1.** the person praying (i.e. the human conduit of God's power), as well as **2.** the recipient of the healing. So receiving a healing via a human conduit involves a combination of faith. Needless to say, there's power in agreement (Matthew 18:20 & Leviticus 26:8). However...
- People with the greatest faith do not require hands to be laid on them for healing or deliverance. This type of faith accepts the LORD at His Word, like the centurion from Matthew 8:5-10,13. In other words, they don't require a human conduit to receive healing or deliverance from God. As noted earlier, the baptism of the Holy Spirit can be received this way (Luke 11:13).

Important Points on Transmitting the Anointing

Here are several things to keep in mind when you lay hands on people to bless, pray, heal or deliver:

- Only make physical contact when you are ready to release your faith.

- While praying over someone you will sense your faith reaching its peak; that's when you should make contact.
- Children may freak out a bit when you lay hands on them because the anointing—God's power—is new to them, but don't let it derail you. Be at peace and keep ministering in faith, as led of the Holy Spirit.
- God's anointing is like electricity flowing through you; your hand is the conductor for this power like an electricity cable.
- When you experience the anointing you'll naturally get excited, which is great; just be careful not to *absorb it* through excessive shouting, laughing and leaping; rather *channel it* to those who need it. In short, don't waste the anointing—get your hands on someone!
- Since your words and hands are the primary vehicles in which the Spirit transmits the anointing to others don't waste words or motions. Watch your words and actions and be careful not to do anything that will drain or lose the anointing, including grieving the Holy Spirit (Ephesians 4:30).
- Put your words and motions in a direct line and use them to bring healing or deliverance to those in need. It's akin to using a rifle: You aim it at the appropriate target in order to hit it. Wasting words and motions will cause you to miss the target.
- If you want God's power to operate strongly in your life, as was the case with The Christ (Acts 10:38), you must discipline yourself to spend time with the LORD. In other words, saturate yourself with God through praise, worship, the Word and prayer. You can't run around gabbing and doing frivolous things—watching TV, playing golf or computer games, etc.—right before a ministry engagement and expect the anointing to be strong when you minister.

- The anointing flows out of your inmost being like rivers of living water out of the very core of your soul/spirit (John 7:37-39). As such, you must protect the anointing so that it'll be there when you need it.
- You can't give something if you don't have it and therefore you can't expect the anointing to flow out of you if you haven't prepared yourself beforehand to operate in God's power. You must never allow people or things to rob you of your worship/Word/prayer time, particularly before you're scheduled to minister. Turn off your phone.

Most Christians unfortunately don't know much about the laying on of hands. This chapter reveals its importance.

5

The RESURRECTION of the Dead

The fifth basic doctrine is the resurrection of the dead, which means that everyone will be bodily resurrected—both the righteous and the unrighteous—as Jesus and Paul plainly declared:

> "for a time is coming when all who are in their graves will hear his voice [29] and come out—those who have done what is good will rise to live, and those who have done what is evil will rise to be condemned."
>
> John 5:28-29

> having hope toward God, which they themselves also wait for, that there is about to be a rising again of the dead, both of righteous and unrighteous;
>
> Acts 24:15 (YLT)

As you can see, there will be resurrections of both the righteous and unrighteous. This doesn't mean, however, that there will only be two resurrections in number, just that there are two *types* of resurrections: **1.** The resurrection of the righteous and **2.** the resurrection of the unrighteous. The former is called "the first resurrection" in Scripture (Revelation 20:5-6), which makes the latter the second resurrection.

The second resurrection takes place at the time of the Great White Throne Judgment, detailed here:

> **Then I saw a great white throne and him who was seated on it. The earth and the heavens fled from his presence, and there was no place for them. [12] And I saw the dead, great and small, standing before the throne, and books were opened. Another book was opened, which is the book of life. The dead were judged according to what they had done as recorded in the books. [13] The sea gave up the dead that were in it, and death and Hades gave up the dead that were in them, and each person was judged according to what they had done. [14] Then death and Hades were thrown into the lake of fire. The lake of fire is the second death. [15] Anyone whose name was not found written in the book of life was thrown into the lake of fire.**
>
> **Revelation 20:11-15**

This massive resurrection and judgment concerns every dead soul contained in Hades (Sheol) after the thousand-year reign of Christ on this earth, which means it involves every unredeemed person throughout history. It does not include Old Testament holy people because they had a covenant with the LORD and will be resurrected after the 7-year Tribulation and before the Millennium (Matthew 19:28-30 & Daniel 12:1-2).

We'll examine the judgment of these unsaved people when we cover the sixth basic doctrine, eternal judgment, next chapter.

The Resurrection of the Righteous

The first resurrection is the resurrection of the righteous, meaning those in right-standing with God. Again, when Jesus and Paul spoke of two basic resurrections they were talking about *types* of resurrections and not numbers. While there's only one resurrection of the unrighteous, the resurrection of the righteous takes place in stages, which correspond to the analogy of a harvest.

In biblical times the harvest took place in three basic stages: **1.** the firstfruits, **2.** the main harvest, and **3.** the gleanings. The harvest began with the firstfruits, which concerned the first fruits and grains to ripen in the season and were offered to the LORD as a sacrifice of thanksgiving (Exodus 23:16,19). Later came the general harvest (Exodus 23:16) and, lastly, the gleanings, which were leftovers for the poor and needy (Leviticus 19:9-10).

Let's examine **the three stages** of the resurrection of the righteous:

1. The Firstfruits. Paul described Jesus as the firstfruits here:

> **But Christ has indeed been raised from the dead, the firstfruits of those who have fallen asleep.** [21] **For since death came through a man, the resurrection of the dead comes also through a man.** [22] **For as in Adam all die, so in Christ all will be made alive.** [23] **But each in turn: Christ, the firstfruits; then, when he comes, those who belong to him.**
>
> 1 Corinthians 15:21-23

Just as the firstfruits of the harvest were a sacrifice to the LORD so Jesus Christ was sacrificed for our sins and raised to life for our justification (Romans 4:25); hence, He's the firstfruits of the resurrection of the righteous.

2. The General Harvest. Verse 23 shows that the main harvest takes place when Jesus returns for the Church—his "bride"—which is the Rapture, detailed in 1 Thessalonians 4:13-18. This harvest includes physically-alive believers translated to heaven.

3. The Gleanings refer to the righteous who were not included in the main harvest and are, as such, "leftovers." This resurrection takes place at the time of Jesus' return at the end of the Tribulation. This return to earth to establish His millennial reign is separate from the Rapture, which is when the general harvest occurs. Remember, when Christ comes for his Church he doesn't return to earth, but rather meets believers in the sky (1 Thessalonians 4:17). We'll address this in a forthcoming section. The gleanings include the resurrection of Old Testament saints as well as the bodily resurrection of believers who died during the Tribulation.

The "gleanings" will also include believers who physically die during the Millennium. Some argue that such a resurrection won't be necessary because, as Isaiah 65:19-25 shows, lifespans will return to the lengthy durations of people before the flood, like Adam and Methuselah. However, this passage doesn't actually say righteous people won't die during the Millennium; notice what it says:

> **Never again will there be in it [Jerusalem] an infant who lives but a few days, or an old man who does not live out his years; the one who dies at a hundred will be thought a mere child; the**

> one who fails to reach a hundred will be considered accursed.
>
> Isaiah 65:20

The passage simply shows that lifespans will be greatly increased, as before the flood; it doesn't say righteous people won't die. In fact, it's implied that blessed people will die by the reference to "an old man who does not live out his years." Moreover, verse 22 says that God's people will live as long as trees during the Millennium. Depending on the species, trees can live less than a hundred years or up to a few thousand, but they ultimately die.

Something else to consider: While it's true that many people lived to be over 900 years old before the flood, it's still not a thousand years, which is how long the Millennium will last. Also, some people died well short of 900-plus years; for instance, Lamech died at 777.

Someone might argue: How can both the resurrection of the righteous at the beginning of the Millennium and another resurrection at the end be "gleanings" since they're separated by a thousand years? Answer: Because the very word "gleanings" implies more than one gleaning; after all, the poor gleaned the harvested fields more than once in biblical times. Also, Psalm 90:4 and 2 Peter 3:8 show that a thousand years is like a day to the LORD, so the two gleanings occur only one day apart from the Divine perspective.

Why is it called the "First Resurrection"?

The resurrection of the righteous is called the "first resurrection" in this passage:

> I saw thrones on which were seated those who had been given authority to judge. And I saw the souls of those who had been beheaded because of their testimony about Jesus and because of the word of God. They had not worshiped the beast or its image and had not received its mark on their foreheads or their hands. They came to life and reigned with Christ a thousand years. [5] (The rest of the dead did not come to life until the thousand years were ended.) <u>This is the first resurrection</u>. [6] Blessed and holy are those who share in <u>the first resurrection</u>. The second death has no power over them, but they will be priests of God and of Christ and will reign with him for a thousand years.
>
> Revelation 20:4-6

The passage refers specifically to the bodily resurrection of Christian martyrs from the Tribulation, which John calls the "first resurrection." By calling it the first resurrection is he saying that there were no resurrections before this? No, because Jesus Christ was resurrected at the beginning of the Church Age and believers will be resurrected bodily at the time of the Rapture while living believers will be translated; not to mention the resurrections of Enoch, Elijah and Moses as types (covered in Chapter Nine of *SHEOL KNOW*). Speaking of those three, their resurrections can be considered "taste-testing of the fruit" according to the harvest analogy.

Here's a diagram that helps visualize the first and second resurrections and the three stages of the first:

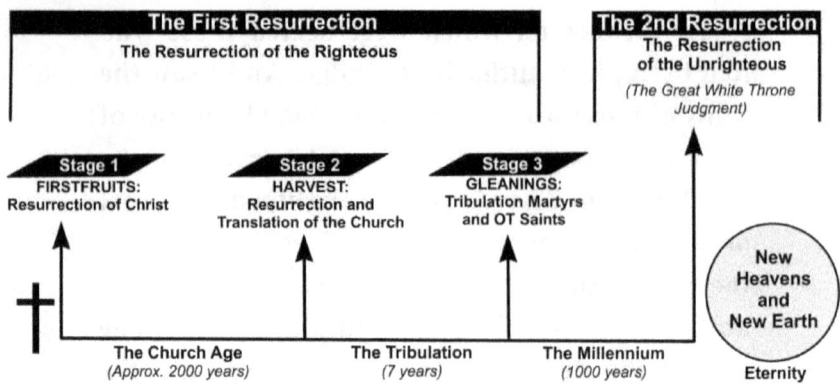

By calling the resurrection of the righteous the "first resurrection" John may mean more than just first in order. The Greek word for "first" is *prótos (PRO-toss)*, which also means principle, chief, honorable or most important. How is the resurrection of the righteous the more honorable resurrection? Because it entails the resurrection of people in right-standing with the LORD through covenant and spiritual rebirth (Titus 3:5 & Ephesians 4:22-24). Since this resurrection involves people who are in right-standing with their Creator, i.e. God's children, it's the more honorable resurrection and therefore the more important one to the LORD, just as the resurrection of your child would be more important to you than the resurrection of some stranger you never knew.

Someone might argue that all people are God's children, even atheists. No, all people are creations of God, but only those born-again of the seed (sperm) of Jesus Christ by the Holy Spirit are children of God (1 John 3:9 & 1 Peter 1:23). Because of the death and resurrection of the Messiah, Old Testament saints who were in covenant with God automatically become spiritually-regenerated at the time of their resurrection.

'Isn't this Too Complicated?'

Some might argue that the resurrection of the righteous—as just mapped out—is too complicated. This is perhaps one of the main reasons why the so-called "father of orthodoxy," Augustine of Hippo, simplified human eschatology by inventing (or, at least, popularizing) the false doctrine of amillennialism. Believe it or not, this erroneous teaching suggests that we're currently *already in* both the Millennium and Tribulation; and when believers or unbelievers die their (supposed) immortal souls[3] either go to heaven forever or suffer never-ending torment in hell. Incredibly, Augustine argued that biblical references to the new Jerusalem, new earth, new heavens and the believer's new glorified body are all symbolic language for heaven! Talk about adding to and taking away from the Holy Scriptures, a practice repeatedly denounced in the Bible (see Revelation 22:18-19, Proverbs 30:6 and Deuteronomy 4:2).[4]

Getting back to our question: Is the resurrection of the dead too complicated? Think about it like this: When referencing a complex subject to someone who knows little on the topic it's best to state the facts in simple terms, which is how Jesus and Paul noted the resurrection of the dead in John 5:28-29 and Acts 24:15 (both cited earlier). Daniel did the same thing in Daniel 12:1-2. All three of these passages detail that there will be a resurrection of both the righteous and the unrighteous, which is true, but they don't go any

---

[3] I say "supposed" immortal souls because the Bible says point blank that **immortality & eternal life are only available through Christ** (2 Timothy 1:10 & Romans 2:7). Immortality is not something people intrinsically possess *apart from* Christ.

[4] See the unabridged version of *HELL KNOW* for more information on Augustine and his false doctrines that corrupted the Church, specifically Chapter Seven's *The Augustinian Corruption of Christendom* and Chapter Nine's *The Good and Bad of Orthodoxy and Traditionalism*.

further than this. As such, we have to look to the rest of Scripture for more details and that's what we're doing here. This is in line with the hermeneutical rule "Scripture interprets Scripture" wherein the more clear and detailed passages offer necessary data that helps interpret the more ambiguous and sketchy ones.

Furthermore, the argument that "this is just too complicated" implies that truth—reality—must always be simple when this just isn't the case. Take brain surgery, for example. Is it simple or does it take years of schooling to master? How about computer technology, astronomy, world history, languages or law? How simple is the road system of any major city? How about the electrical grid of New York City? I could go on and on.

Yes, the resurrection of the dead is more complicated than what Augustine taught, but it's certainly not too complicated for the average person to grasp. The above diagram illustrates that it's actually not that complicated and it's much less complicated than any of the topics just listed.

The resurrection of the dead is cited as one of the six basic doctrines of Christianity in Hebrews 6:1-2. The writer of Hebrews was lamenting that the people he was addressing needed to be taught these basic doctrines all over again when they should've been teachers by this point (Hebrews 5:11-12). Now, think about it: If the topic of the resurrection of the dead was as simple as Augustine taught—that is, people just go to heaven or hell when they die to spend eternity in either bliss or torment—why would these people need to be taught the subject again? If the subject were that simplistic it'd take just a few minutes to teach and not a whole sermon or series of sermons. Moreover, if it were that simple how could the believers not grasp it the first time around?

Yes, the resurrection of the dead is a complicated subject, so what? That's why it needs taught properly and thoroughly.

Jesus' Rapture of the Church and Return to Earth

I pointed out something earlier that should be elaborated: Most believers don't realize that there are two phases to the Lord's Second Coming: **1.** Christ's return for his Church, known as the Rapture, and **2.** Christ's return to the earth to establish his millennial kingdom. The former is detailed in 1 Thessalonians 4:13-18 and the latter in Revelation 19:11-16. A comparison of these passages and other pertinent Scriptures reveal two separate phases of Jesus' Second Coming that can be distinguished like so:

The Lord's Second Coming	
PHASE 1 The Rapture (1 Thessalonians 4:13-18)	PHASE 2 Christ's Return to the Earth (Revelation 19:11-16)
Christ appears in the air	Christ returns to the earth
Jesus returns in secret, like a thief	Jesus returns openly
The Messiah returns *for* his Church	Messiah returns *with* his Church
The Lord comes as Bridegroom	The Lord comes as King
Christ comes as deliverer	Christ comes as warrior and judge
Jesus comes with grace	Jesus comes with grace and wrath
The Messiah delivers the Church *from* wrath	Messiah delivers believers (of the Tribulation) who endured wrath
Living believers receive immortal bodies as they are taken to heaven	Living believers remain mortal on the earth during the Millennium
The world is left unjudged	The world is judged (Mt. 25:31-46)
The world continues in sin	Righteousness is established
Addresses only the saved	Addresses the saved and unsaved
Can happen at any moment	Many signs must first occur
The devil continues his evil reign	The devil is cast into the Abyss

One of the differences on the list is that the Lord's return for his Church—the Rapture—can happen at any time once the general season of the end is apparent, meaning it's **imminent**, whereas many distinct signs precede Christ's return to the earth. These signs include, amongst others: the global cataclysm of the Tribulation period itself (Revelation 6-19), the revealing of the antichrist (2 Thessalonians 2:1-8), the two witnesses (Revelation 11:1-12) and the institution of the mark of the beast (Revelation 13:16-17). Generally speaking, once the Tribulation begins—and it will be obvious when it does—you can be sure that Jesus will return to the earth seven years later (which is different than saying you'll be able to pinpoint the precise moment or day).

However, this isn't the case with the Lord's return for his Church because, again, it's imminent and could happen at any time with zero warning once the general season of his return is at hand, which means *now* (Matthew 24:3-14). Notice what Jesus said:

> [36] **"But about that day or hour no one knows, not even the angels in heaven, nor the Son, but only the Father.** [37] **As it was in the days of Noah, so it will be at the coming of the Son of Man...**
> [42] **"Therefore keep watch, because you do not know on what day your Lord will come.** [43] **But understand this: If the owner of the house had known at what time of night the thief was coming, he would have kept watch and would not have let his house be broken into.** [44] **So you also must be ready, because the Son of Man will come at an hour when you do not expect him.**
> **Matthew 24:36-37, 42-44**

As you can see, we are instructed to "keep watch" and "be ready" because Jesus "will come at an hour when we do not expect him."

Interestingly, the Son doesn't even know the day or hour, only the Father knows (verse 36). We must be "dressed ready for service" and "keep our lamps burning" (Luke 12:35) precisely because the Lord's return for his Church is imminent. I should add that, while we don't know the day or hour, we can know the general season via Jesus' descriptions and, again, that season is now.

While some claim that the word "Rapture" isn't biblical, it is. It refers to a phrase used in this passage:

> **After that, we who are still alive and are left will be <u>caught up</u> together with them in the clouds to meet the Lord in the air. And so we will be with the Lord forever.**
> **1 Thessalonians 4:17**

'Caught up' in the Greek is *harpazó (har-PAD-zoh)*, which means to "snatch up" or "obtain by robbery." It's translated in Latin as "rapio" in the Vulgate, which is where we get the English "Rapture." With this understanding, when our "Bridegroom" (Jesus) comes for his "bride" (the Church) he's going to obtain us by **robbing us off the earth**!

The aforementioned 1 Thessalonians 4:13-18 is the most prominent support text for the Rapture:

> **Brothers and sisters, we do not want you to be uninformed about those who sleep in death, so that you do not grieve like the rest of mankind, who have no hope. [14] For we believe that Jesus died and rose again, and so we believe that God will bring with Jesus those who have fallen asleep in him. [15] According to the Lord's word, we tell you that we who are still alive, who are**

left until <u>the coming of the Lord</u>, will certainly not precede those who have fallen asleep. ¹⁶ For <u>the Lord himself will come down from heaven</u>, with a loud command, with the voice of the archangel and with the trumpet call of God, and <u>the dead in Christ will rise first</u>. ¹⁷ After that, <u>we who are still alive and are left will be caught up together with them in the clouds to meet the Lord in the air</u>. And so we will be with the Lord forever. ¹⁸ Therefore encourage each other with these words.

1 Thessalonians 4:13-18

Here's more support:

"Do not let your hearts be troubled. You believe in God; believe also in me. ² My Father's house has many rooms; if that were not so, would I have told you that I am going there to prepare a place for you? ³ And if I go and prepare a place for you, <u>I will come back and take you to be with me that you also may be where I am</u>."

John 14:1-3

Listen, I tell you a mystery: We will not all sleep, but we <u>will all be changed</u>—⁵² <u>in a flash, in the twinkling of an eye</u>, at the last trumpet. For the trumpet will sound, <u>the dead will be raised imperishable, and we will be changed</u>.

1 Corinthians 15:51-52

and <u>to wait for his Son from heaven</u>, whom he raised from the dead—<u>Jesus, who rescues us from the coming wrath</u>.

1 Thessalonians 1:10

What is the "coming wrath" in this context and how does Jesus "rescue" us from it? The coming wrath refers to the seven-year Tribulation and the Lord rescues the Church from it via the Rapture, which Paul elaborates on shortly later in his epistle (4:13-18).

Notice what Christ promises the faithful church of Philadelphia:

> **"Since you have kept my command to endure patiently, <u>I will also keep you from the hour of trial that is going to come on the whole world</u> to test the inhabitants of the earth."**
>
> **Revelation 3:10**

"The hour of trial that is going to come on the whole world" is referring to the Tribulation period detailed in Revelation 6-19. Jesus doesn't say he would just protect believers during the Tribulation, but that he'd "keep them from the hour of trial" altogether. Keep in mind that, while the church at Philadelphia was one of seven 1st century churches that Christ addresses in Revelation 2-3, these seven churches were picked by the Lord because they *typify* the seven kinds of assemblies that exist throughout the Church Age. As such, Jesus' words were to all faithful Christians throughout the ensuing centuries of the Church Age. In fact, since the Rapture and the Tribulation didn't come at the general time of this message to the church of Philadelphia circa 90-100 AD, the passage must *more specifically* apply to a future generation of faithful believers.

Further support for the Rapture can be observed in what happens to John in the book of Revelation. Christ gave John the threefold contents of Revelation at the end of chapter 1: "Write, therefore, **what you have seen, what is now** and **what will take place later**" (Revelation 1:19). This is the Contents Page of the book of

Revelation: "What you have seen" refers to chapter 1 because that's what John had seen up to that point in the vision while "what is now" refers to chapters 2-3 and "what will take place later" refers to chapters 4-22.

Chapters 2-3 of Revelation cover "what is now," meaning the Church Age, as noted above. These chapters cover the seven types of assemblies that exist throughout the Church Age. Chapters 4-22 address "what will take place later" and chapters 4-19 specifically the period of the Tribulation, which involves the seal, trumpet and bowl judgments of God's wrath that will befall the earth and its inhabitants.

Here's my point: John was an apostle of the Church and right at the opening of Revelation 4—which is the beginning of his coverage of the Tribulation—Jesus says to him, "Come up here," referring to heaven (verse 1). You see? John is representative of the Church and just before the Tribulation he is taken up into heaven. Why? Because the Church itself will be delivered from the Tribulation via Christ's return for his Church, which is the Rapture.

Another thing to consider is that the Church is referred to no less than nineteen times in the first three chapters of Revelation and not once on earth in chapters 4-19. Why? Because the existing Church—all genuine believers—will be "snatched up" to heaven before the Tribulation starts. Revelation 19 details Christ's return to the earth at the end of the Tribulation. Guess who's riding with him? The Church (verse 14; also verified by 1 Thessalonians 4:14).

This doesn't mean, however, that there won't be believers during the Tribulation because there will be multitudes; and, yes, they are the Church because 'church' simply refers to the *ekklesia (ek-klay-SEE-ah)*, the "called-out ones" who are called out of the darkness of this world into the kingdom of light. However, the *existing* Church at the time of the Rapture before the Tribulation will have been snatched away. In other words, believers during the Tribulation are those who embrace the gospel *after* the Rapture. We'll address this in the next section.

The snatching up of the Church before the Tribulation corresponds to the biblical pattern of the righteous being saved from destruction when God's judgment falls on unrepentant masses. Jesus noted this pattern when he taught on the Rapture:

> **For the Son of Man in his day will be like the lightning, which flashes and lights up the sky from one end to the other. [25] But first he must suffer many things and be rejected by this generation.**
> **[26] "<u>Just as it was</u> in the days of Noah, <u>so also will it be</u> in the days of the Son of Man. [27] People were eating, drinking, marrying and being given in marriage up to the day Noah entered the ark. Then the flood came and destroyed them all.**
> **[28] "<u>It was the same</u> in the days of Lot. People were eating and drinking, buying and selling, planting and building. [29] But the day Lot left Sodom, fire and sulfur rained down from heaven and destroyed them all.**
> **[30] "<u>It will be just like this on the day the Son of Man is revealed</u>. [31] On that day no one who is on the housetop, with possessions inside, should go down to get them. Likewise, no one in the field should go back for anything. [32] Remember Lot's wife! [33] Whoever tries to keep their life will lose it, and whoever loses their life will preserve it. [34] I tell you, on that night two people will be in one**

> bed; one will be taken and the other left. [35] Two women will be grinding grain together; one will be taken and the other left."
>
> Luke 17:24-35

Christ is talking about "the day the Son of Man is revealed" (verse 30) that "will be like the lightning, which flashes and lights up the sky from one end to the other" (verse 24). In other words, it'll take place in the blink of an eye. The last two verses show beyond any shadow of doubt that Jesus was talking about His snatching up of the Church: "Two people will be in bed; one will be taken and the other left. Two women will be grinding grain together; one will be taken and the other left" (verses 34-35). This, incidentally, presents a problem for those who argue that the Rapture takes place at the same time as Jesus' return to the earth at the end of the Tribulation because the impression of these verses is that of ordinary everyday life and not of people who just went through a worldwide cataclysm horrifically described in Revelation 6-19 wherein three quarters of the population of the earth will perish.

Observe in verses 26-29 how Jesus likens the time of the Rapture to the "days of Noah" and the "days of Lot." "Just as it was" in the days of these two "so it will be" when Christ returns for his Church. What's the significance of this? In the days of Noah and Lot there were warnings of the LORD's coming judgment on masses of people if they stubbornly refused to repent. In Noah's situation the judgment concerned the entire world whereas in Lot's situation it concerned the cities of Sodom and Gomorrah. In both cases **the righteous were removed *before* God's judgment fell**. "So it will be" with the future Tribulation—those in right-standing with the Lord will be taken out of the way *before* God's wrath falls on rebellious humanity. Those who become believers during the Tribulation are those who wisely respond to the pouring out of God's wrath by repenting & believing.

In verse 30 Jesus says "It will be just like this on the day the Son of Man is revealed." Just like what? Just like the days of Noah and Lot where people were carrying on business as usual—eating, drinking, marrying, buying, selling, planting and building (verses 27-28). This is what people will be doing when Christ comes for his Church, not enduring a global upheaval, which disproves the post-Tribulation position.

Speaking of the post-Tribulation view, how do people who hold this position explain Luke 17:24-35? They argue that Jesus only speaks of his coming once in this passage, not twice, and when he comes he will **1.** snatch up the righteous and then **2.** pour out his wrath on the unrighteous, citing verses 26-32. The problem with this, of course, is that **it's an explicit description of the pre-Tribulation position** (or, at least, "pre-wrath"). The only thing they're omitting is Christ's return to the earth after God's wrath is poured out on rebellious humanity to set up his millennial kingdom (Matthew 25:31). As already explained, this is detailed in the book of Revelation: In Revelation 4:1 Jesus says to John—representing the Church—to "come up here" to heaven. Chapters 4-19 cover the Tribulation where God's wrath is poured out and Jesus returns to the earth at the end (Revelation 19).

Here's a timeline diagram to help visualize these events:

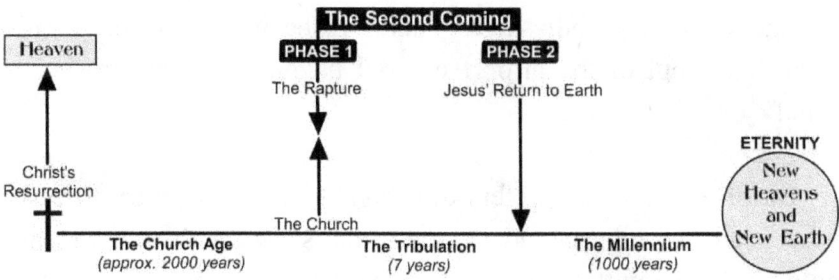

Some people suggest that the Rapture isn't part of Jesus' Second Coming and that only His return to the earth should be designated as the Second coming, but Christ himself spoke of his snatching up of the Church as "the coming of the Son of Man" (Matthew 24:27,37,39) and within this context are clear references to the Tribulation (verses 21-22 & 29). The Greek for "coming" in these passages is *parousia (par-oo-SEE-ah)*, traditionally translated as "advent" in Christian circles, as in "the Second Advent of Christ." This is **the same word** used to describe the Lord's coming at the end of the Tribulation in 2 Thessalonians 2:8. Jesus elsewhere referred to this latter coming as "When the Son of Man comes in his glory" (Matthew 16:27 & 25:31). Since the Rapture of the Church is clearly separate from the Lord's coming to the earth—with the Tribulation separating them—and both the Rapture and Christ's return to the earth are described in terms of "coming" (*parousia*) then we must conclude that they both represent his Second Coming, albeit two phases.

Someone might argue: "But these two phases are separated by several years, how can both refer to the same Second Coming? Because it's **one coming taking place in two stages**. Besides, seven years isn't that long of a time to the eternal God. Let me put it in perspective: The Bible says that a thousand years is like a day to the Lord (Psalm 90:4 & 2 Peter 3:8), which means that seven years would be like 10½ minutes! So from Jesus' perspective the Second Coming—both stages—takes place in 10½ minutes. It's hard to get out of the airport without baggage in that amount of time!

If you or anyone else prefers to designate Christ's return to earth specifically as his Second Coming, that's fine with me. I'm not going to argue with you. But this doesn't change the biblical fact that *parousia* is used to describe BOTH **1.** Christ's rapture of the Church and **2.** his return to earth shortly later. Furthermore, consider this: To believers the rapture IS Christ's Second Coming whereas to the unsaved his return to earth is His Second Coming. So both refer to His Second Coming depending upon the spiritual condition of the individual; they're just two different phases.

Lastly, notice what this passage says:

> **so Christ was sacrificed once to take away the sins of many; and <u>he will appear a second time</u>, not to bear sin, but <u>to bring salvation to those who are waiting for him</u>.**
> **Hebrews 9:28**

As you can see, the verse states that Christ will appear "a second time"—clearly referring to his Second Coming—and then goes on to say that when he appears this "second time" he will "bring salvation to those who are waiting for him," which is an obvious reference to **the Rapture**.

"For it will Not be, Unless the Departure Comes First"

Both phases of the Lord's Second Coming are covered in this passage:

> **Now, brothers, <u>concerning the coming of our Lord Jesus Christ, and our gathering together to him</u>, we ask you ² not to be quickly shaken in your mind, nor yet be troubled, either by spirit, or by word, or by letter as from us, saying that the day of Christ had come. ³ Let no one deceive you in any way. For it will not be, unless the departure comes first, and the man of sin is**

revealed, the son of destruction, ⁴ who opposes and exalts himself against all that is called God or that is worshiped; so that he sits as God in the temple of God, setting himself up as God. ⁵ Don't you remember that, when I was still with you, I told you these things? ⁶ Now you know what is restraining him, to the end that he may be revealed in his own season. ⁷ For the mystery of lawlessness already works. Only there is one who restrains now, until he is taken out of the way. ⁸Then the lawless one will be revealed, <u>whom the Lord will kill with the breath of his mouth, and destroy by the manifestation of his coming;</u>

2 Thessalonians 2:1-8 (WEB)

Verse 1 shows that this text concerns the Second Coming, including the Church being "gathered together to him," which is the Rapture. Verse 8 details the second phase of Christ's coming, which is when he returns to the earth and destroys the "lawless one"—the antichrist—with a mere word or two from his lips. (So much for Christ being a milksop weakling as he's often maligned in modern Western culture!) The Greek word for "coming" in both verses is the aforementioned *parousia*. You see? The Second Coming consists of **1.** Jesus' return for his Church and **2.** His return to the earth to vanquish his enemies and establish his millennial kingdom.

Verse 3 reveals the sequence of events, emphasizing that the "day of Christ" will not come to pass until "the departure comes first, and the man of sin is revealed." The "departure" is an obvious reference to the snatching up of the Church while the revealing of the "man of sin" refers to the unveiling of the antichrist, a wicked, possessed man who will obtain worldwide power during the Tribulation (Revelation 13:7).

The Greek word for "departure" is *apostasia (ap-os-tas-EE-ah)* and is only used one other time in the Bible where it refers to departing from the law of Moses (Acts 21:21). Interestingly, the word was translated as "departure" or "departing" in 2 Thessalonians 2:3 in the first seven English translations of the Bible, which changed when the King James translators decided to translate it as "falling away." Most modern English versions have followed suit by translating it as "apostasy" or "rebellion," but the World English Bible (above) translates it as "departure." I believe this is the proper translation for a few reasons:

1. The verb form of the word is used 14 times in the New Testament where it predominantly means "departed." Luke 2:37 is a good example where it refers to an elderly prophetess who "never *left* the temple but worshiped night and day, fasting and praying;" Acts 12:10 is another example where it refers to an angel *leaving* Peter after helping him escape from prison.
2. It doesn't make sense in the context of 2 Thessalonians 2:3 to translate *apostasia* as "rebellion" or "apostasy"/"falling away." Concerning the former, the world has always been in rebellion against genuine Christianity (please notice I said "genuine"). Concerning the latter, there's already mass apostasy in Christendom with whole denominations embracing gross libertinism and rejecting the most obvious biblical axioms. In fact, this has been increasing for decades.
3. Translating *apostasia* as "departure" fits both the immediate context of 2 Thessalonians 2:1-8 and the greater context of the Lord's Second Coming in the Bible, the latter of which we've already covered. Concerning the former, verse 1 speaks of the Second Coming in terms of the Church being gathered to Jesus, which involves believers *departing from* this earth. And verses 6-8 speak of

the "restrainer" of lawlessness, which must be removed before the antichrist can rise to power. Who is this "restrainer" of lawlessness? The most obvious answer is the Holy Spirit and, by extension, the Church, which is the **temple of the Holy Spirit** (1 Corinthians 3:16). When they depart the earth the antichrist will no longer be restrained and, in the vacuum, will make his move. Whereas the Church will remain in heaven during the Tribulation the Holy Spirit will return as masses of wise people will almost immediately turn to God after the incredible testimony of the Rapture. The Holy Spirit obviously returns because it's the Spirit who regenerates people through the gospel (Titus 3:5). Untold millions will be saved during the Tribulation (Revelation 7:9,14) through the testimony of **A.** the Rapture, **B.** the 144,000 Jewish evangelists, **C.** the two witnesses, **D.** the mass divine judgments, and **E.** an angel commissioned to preach the eternal gospel to the inhabitants of the earth (Revelation 14:6-7).

As you can see, 2 Thessalonians 2:1-8 strongly supports the two phases of the Second Coming and the pre-Tribulation Rapture.

Let me close by stressing that I personally don't care if the Rapture takes place before the Tribulation, mid-Tribulation or "pre-wrath." I don't even care if it takes place at the same general time as Christ's return to the earth at the end of the Tribulation. Don't get me wrong, like any sane believer I have zero desire to go through the Tribulation, but as a responsible minister of the Word of God all I care about is accurately conveying what the Bible teaches; and my studies have led me to conclude what is contained in these last two sections. Bear in mind that I'm a devoted non-sectarian and therefore don't draw doctrinal conclusions based on the pressure of a certain group. I draw conclusions from the God-breathed

Scriptures and, as you see, they overwhelmingly point in the direction of a pre-Tribulation Rapture.

I encourage you to unbiasedly look at the different perspectives in your studies and draw your own conclusions with the help of the Holy Spirit. I recommend the works of David Reagan, Hal Lindsey and Todd Strandberg on this topic.

Lastly, all genuine believers who know how to read agree that the Lord will "snatch up" his Church when he returns based on the clear passages we've looked at in this section, so the Rapture is a biblical fact. It's the *timing* of the Rapture that believers disagree on and this is a secondary issue; it's not something to heatedly argue about or break fellowship over. Whether pre, mid, post or pre-wrath, the Rapture will occur.

6

Eternal JUDGMENT

The sixth basic doctrine of Christianity is that all persons will stand before the LORD for assessment and this will have eternal ramifications. The word "eternal" in the Greek is the adjective *aionios (ay-OH-nee-us)*, which is derived from the noun *aion (ay-OHN)*. *Aion* is where we get the English 'eon,' meaning "an age." As such, *aionios* means "like an age" or "age-lasting." Since *aionios* in the phrase "eternal judgment" refers to the coming everlasting age, God's ultimate judgment on people relates to eternity. Are you with me?

Now notice how this verse describes God:

> **There is only one Lawgiver and Judge, the one who is able to <u>save</u> and <u>destroy</u>.**
> **James 4:12**

This is a New Testament passage and it describes the LORD in terms of being a Judge, a Judge who's going to do one of two things with people depending on what they choose to do or not do on earth: He's either going to **save** or **destroy**. Whether salvation or destruction, the judgment is eternal, meaning it applies to the never-ending age to come, which is the age of the new heavens and new earth (2 Peter 3:7,13).

There are four judgments involving people and they apply to: **1.** the unrighteous who have died throughout history (i.e. the lost), **2.** New Covenant believers, **3.** the unsaved still alive when Christ returns to the Earth at the end of the Tribulation and **4.** Old Testament saints. I share them in this order because that's the order we're going to look at them…

The Great White Throne Judgment: Eternal Judgment of the Lost

The eternal judgment of the unredeemed is solemnly detailed in this passage:

> **¹³ The sea gave up the dead that were in it, and death and Hades gave up the dead that were in them, and each person was judged according to what they had done. ¹⁴ Then death and Hades were thrown into the lake of fire. The lake of fire is the second death. ¹⁵ Anyone whose name was not found written in the book of life was thrown into the lake of fire.**
>
> **Revelation 20:13-15**

The LORD's judgment for anyone whose name is not found written in the book of life is being cast into the lake of fire, which is described as the "second death." This is the judgment of the unrepentant wicked spoken of in Hebrews in terms of **"raging fire that will consume the enemies of God"** (Hebrews 10:26-27).

Paul described the second death as "everlasting destruction" (2 Thessalonians 1:9) while Jesus was even more explicit:

> **"Do not be afraid of those who kill the body but cannot kill the soul. Rather, be afraid of the One** [God] **who can <u>destroy both soul and body in hell</u>** *(Gehenna)***."**
>
> Matthew 10:28

God's going to literally destroy the unrepentant wicked in the lake of fire, not preserve them for eternal roasting torture. Christ elsewhere described human damnation in terms of "eternal punishment" (Matthew 25:46) but there's a difference between eternal punishment and eternal punish*ing*. The Greek word for "punishment" is *kolasis (KOL-as-is)*, which refers to a "penal infliction" and is therefore a judicial sentence. Jesus does not say in Matthew 25 what the penal infliction will be, only that it will take place in the lake of fire ("the eternal fire") and that this infliction will last forever (that is, take place in the age-to-come, which lasts forever). Since Christ doesn't specify what exactly the penal sentence is, we must therefore turn to the rest of Scripture for answers. "Scripture interprets Scripture" is an interpretational rule. And we see above that Jesus plainly said God would "destroy both soul and body" in the lake of fire.

For additional evidence, consider these four points that reinforce each other:

1. Christ and the apostles plainly taught what would happen to ungodly people when they suffer "the second death." They taught that:

- the ungodly would **die** (John 11:26 & Romans 8:13),
- that they would experience **death** (John 8:51, Romans 6:23 & James 5:20),
- that **destruction** would occur (Matthew 7:13 & 2 Peter 3:7),
- that both their souls and bodies would be **destroyed** (Matthew 10:28 & James 4:12),
- and that they would **perish** (John 3:16 & 2 Peter 3:9).

As you can see, the Bible continually speaks of the eternal fate of the unrepentant wicked in explicit terms of destruction: "die," "death," "destruction," "destroy" and "perish." I refer to this as the "language of destruction." The Holy Spirit wrote the Scriptures via people of God (2 Peter 1:20-21) and the terminology the Holy Spirit chose to use was the language of **destruction**, not the language of eternal conscious torture.

2. In a desperate effort to repudiate the above, advocates of eternal torture try to claim that the Greek word translated as "destroy" and "perish" in passages like Matthew 10:28 and John 3:16—*apollumi (ah-POHL-loo-mee)*—means "destruction, not of being, but of well-being." However this is easily disproven because Jesus used this very word (as conveyed by Luke) to describe the **incineration** of the people of Sodom (Luke 17:29). Bear in mind that both the Old and New Testaments detail that Sodom & Gomorrah were **burned to ashes** and, even more, that this total incineration is **an example of what will happen to the ungodly on the day of judgment** (2 Peter 2:6). What word did Christ use to describe this incineration in Luke 17:29? Why, *appolumi*, the very same word translated as "destroy" in Matthew 10:28 and "perish" in John 3:16. Enough said.

3. Backing up the above two points are the unmistakable *examples* of literal destruction used in reference to the second death, like weeds thrown into fire and burned (Matthew 13:40). Tell me, what happens to weeds cast into fire? Do they burn forever and ever without ever quite burning up or do they burn for a little while, but ultimately burn up? "Burn up" is incidentally the way John the Baptist described human damnation in Matthew 3:12 and Luke 3:17. Then there's Jesus' example of the enemies of the king (figurative of Christ) being brought before him and **executed in front of him**, not preserved and perpetually tormented in his presence (Luke 19:27). Another great example is that of "hell" itself. The only Greek word translated as "hell" in English Bibles that's applicable to the second death is Gehenna, which literally means Valley of Hinnom or Hinnom Valley. This ravine was a trash dump and incinerator located outside the southwest walls of Jerusalem at the time of Christ. You can see it on close-up maps of Jerusalem in the backs of most Bibles. Jesus used Gehenna as a figure for the lake of fire & human damnation and his listeners readily understood it. Trash and carcasses of animals & despised criminals weren't thrown into Gehenna to be preserved, but rather to **be discarded and eradicated**. It's the same with unrighteous rebels on Judgment Day when they're cast into the lake of fire.

4. The above points are further reinforced by the fact that **eternal life and immortality are only available to people through the gospel of Christ**, as clearly shown in 2 Timothy 1:10 and Romans 2:7. Jesus plainly said that human beings are mortal apart from redemption and that angelic spirits possess intrinsic immortality, even wicked spirits (Luke 20:34-36), which explains why the lake of fire—the "eternal fire"—was "prepared for the devil and his angels" as their eternal habitation (Matthew 25:41). However, human beings are mortal apart from redemption in Christ. The very reason the LORD was sure to banish Adam & Eve from the Garden of Eden was so that they *wouldn't* "eat of the tree of life and live forever" (Genesis 3:22-24) and thus suffer the same fate as the devil and his angels. Only the redeemed will be allowed to "eat of the tree of life" and live forever (Revelation 2:7).

For important details on human damnation (hell) see my book *HELL KNOW*. For details on the nature of Sheol/Hades, the intermediate state of the unsaved dead, see *SHEOL KNOW*. Both of these topics are too huge to go into further detail here.

The Great White Throne Judgment brings up an obvious question: Will every person who partakes of this judgment automatically be cast into the lake of fire? After all, what about those who never heard the gospel? What about those who heard the gospel but didn't understand it for one legitimate reason or another? What about those who rejected it because it was either a flawed, religionized version of the gospel or it came with serious baggage, like imperialism? Every legitimate minister of God's Word must consider these obvious questions and try to answer them based on what the Bible says and simple common sense. I would be seriously skeptical of anyone who doesn't do this, particularly those who write off such questions in preference to the official position of whatever group they adhere to, which is an example of rigid sectarianism. Religious faction-ism like this actually hinders the truth and, in fact, is a form of legalism, i.e. counterfeit Christianity. Remember, Jesus said it's the truth that will set us free (John 8:31-32), so anything that hinders the acquisition of truth is not good. In any case, these questions are explored in the unabridged version of *HELL KNOW*.

The Judgment Seat of Christ

The Judgment Seat of Christ is detailed in these two passages:

> For <u>we</u> [believers] <u>**must all appear before the judgment seat of Christ**</u>, so that each of <u>us</u> may receive what is due <u>us</u> for the things done while in the body, whether good or bad.
> ¹¹ Since, then, <u>we</u> know what it is to fear the Lord, we try to persuade others.
>
> 2 Corinthians 5:10-11

> You, then, why do you judge your brother or sister? Or why do you treat them with contempt? For <u>we</u> [believers] <u>**will all stand before God's judgment seat**</u>... ¹² So then, each of <u>us</u> <u>will give an account of ourselves to God</u>.
>
> Romans 14:10, 12

Paul is **addressing believers** in both passages and he says that *we* must all appear before the Judgment Seat of Christ. This is the judgment that believers will experience and is also called the *Bema (BAY-mah)* Judgment, named after the Greek word for "judgment seat." Christians will not be evaluated at the Great White Throne Judgment, as that particular judgment only concerns spiritually-dead people (Revelation 20:11-15).

The purpose of the Judgment Seat of Christ is obviously not to determine who will be granted eternal life, as all spiritually regenerated believers rightfully possess such. The exceptions would be those proven to be hypocrites, that is, fakes (e.g. Matthew 7:15-23), which we'll honestly look at as we progress. The purpose of this judgment is to acknowledge and reward Christians for the good things they did while in the body and to rebuke and penalize them for the bad, which will include an appraisal of our works. The "bad" will *not* concern sins already confessed because God forgives all such transgressions—*dismisses* them—and purifies us from the corresponding unrighteousness (1 John 1:8-9).

The "bad" would include both unconfessed sins of commission and sins of omission. A sin of commission is something we *do*, like gossip and slander. A sin of omission involves something we *don't* do that we should have done. For instance, if God prompts a lady to give someone in need $100 and she doesn't do it; or if the LORD calls a lawyer into full-time ministry and he ignores the call. These are sins of omission.

There's something in the first passage above that we need to consider: After stating that Christians will receive what is due them for the good or bad things they did, the apostle Paul adds in verse 11: "Since then, we know what it is to fear the Lord." The King James Version translates this as "Knowing therefore the terror of the Lord." This statement makes zero sense *if* believers just receive rewards at the Judgment Seat of Christ, as I've heard some ministers erroneously teach. Knowing that Christians will be held accountable for the bad things they do in this life can inspire some healthy "terror." For those of us who are Christians, it's spiritually healthy to regularly remind ourselves that we will one day stand before the throne of God and give an accounting of our lives, which is why the writer of Hebrews stressed it (Hebrews 4:13). Needless to say, the fear of the Lord inspires holy (pure) living. It inspires humbly "keeping with repentance" when we miss it (Matthew & Luke 3:8).

A minister argued that the Greek word for "bad" in 2 Corinthians 5:10 doesn't refer to moral evil and so, he claimed, believers won't be held accountable for unconfessed sins, including sins of omission. He argued that the word only means "worthless," such as a piece of fruit that's rotten. Actually the Greek word for "bad" *can* refer to moral evil, as well as something worthless. The word is *phaulos (FOW-los)*. Observe how Christ plainly uses this word in reference to moral evil:

> "For everyone who does <u>evil</u> *(phaulos)* hates the Light, and does not come to the Light for fear that his deeds will be exposed."
>
> John 3:20 (NAS)

> "Do not marvel at this; for an hour is coming, in which all who are in the tombs will hear His voice, and will come forth; those who did the good deeds to a resurrection of life, those who committed <u>the evil deeds</u> *(phaulos)* to a resurrection of judgment."
>
> John 5:29 (NAS)

Interestingly, *phaulos* appears only six times in the Greek Scriptures and it's translated as either "bad" or "evil" and not once as "worthless." Chew on that.

The good news is that God "is faithful and just and will **forgive us our sins** and **purify us from all unrighteousness**" whenever we humbly 'fess up (1 John 1:9), which means that we will *not* be culpable for these transgressions at the Judgment Seat. This is a spur to "keep in repentance" (Matthew & Luke 3:8).

The Greek word for 'judgment' in reference to the sixth basic doctrine—"eternal judgment" (Hebrews 6:2)—is *krima (KREE-mah)*, which means "judgment, verdict or lawsuit." The Greek for 'judgment seat' in the phrase "judgment seat of Christ" is a different word, the aforementioned *bema*, which refers to a platform or throne from which justice is administered.

Because of this, some might suggest that the sixth basic doctrine—eternal judgment—doesn't apply to believers, but it does. For instance, James 3:1 says that "Not many of you should become teachers, my fellow believers, because you know that we who teach will be *judged* more strictly." James was addressing believers and says that those who teach will be judged more sternly. More literal translations say they will "receive a stricter judgment" (e.g. NASB and NKJV). The word "judgment" (or "judged" in the NIV) is the aforementioned *krima* used in the phrase "eternal judgment" in Hebrews 6:2. Where do you suppose those who teach God's Word will experience this stricter judgment? Not the Great White Throne Judgment, since that judgment applies strictly to *un*believers. No, these teachers will be judged at the Judgment Seat of Christ, which is where Christians are appraised.

Note what the Lord says in this verse:

> **"Anyone who speaks a word against the Son of Man [Jesus] will be forgiven, but anyone who speaks against the Holy Spirit will not be forgiven, either in this age or the age to come."**
> **Matthew 12:32**

The implication is that some sins—sins *not* confessed and forgiven **in this age**—must be dealt with and forgiven **in the age to come**. We will be held accountable for these sins at the Judgment Seat, penalized and ultimately forgiven. This does not in any way mean that the sufferings of Christ were insufficient to save us. All of our sins that are "under the blood" are forgiven; it's the sins that are not "under the blood" when we die that must be dealt with at the Bema Judgment.

Someone might argue that Jesus died on the cross for our past, present *and* future sins and therefore it's not technically necessary to keep in repentance to be forgiven of sins not yet committed. While it's true that Jesus died for our future sins along with our past and present ones, you can't very well confess something you haven't even done yet, which is why 1 John 1:8-9 is in the Bible, as well as similar passages, like Proverbs 28:13 (also see 2 Corinthians 12:21). Those who die with unconfessed sin will have to answer for these sins at the Judgment Seat since they were not confessed and forgiven—dismissed by the Lord—*before* they physically died. Because these offenses weren't dismissed they'll be accountable to them. While believers won't have to suffer the ultimate wage of sin since Christ paid the penalty of death in our place, they will be penalized as the Lord dictates at the Judgment Seat wherein there are two basic types of penalties, which we'll look at as we progress.

Some object to the notion of believers being judged on the grounds that Christ returns "to bring salvation to those who are waiting for him" and (supposedly) not to judge them (Hebrews 9:28). Yes, the Lord is returning to bring salvation to believers, but this does not negate the reality and necessity of the Bema Judgment.

I know believers who routinely rip off people in business or readily engage in gossip & slander, usually due to hidden (but obvious) envy, rivalry and malice. The latter poisons listeners' minds against fellow believers—sometimes believers they've never even met—and this naturally creates division in the body of Christ. The Enemy loves this! What doctrine of demons have these people embraced to cause them to walk in such blatant unrighteousness without repentance? Answer: The false doctrine that believers can sin all they want with no care of repentance and never be held accountable because Jesus is returning to bring salvation to believers and no judgment whatsoever. It's a wicked and thoroughly unbiblical doctrine! The Judgment Seat of Christ is part of the Six Basic Doctrines and is therefore a foundational teaching of genuine Christianity. It inspires God-fearing holiness and a spirit of humble repentance in believers. It protects us from false doctrine, like the idea that believers won't have to stand before the Lord at the Judgment Seat of Christ and give an account. Hebrews 4:13 says differently (look it up).

Appraising the Believer's Works at the Judgment Seat

As noted, the Bema Judgment will include an appraisal of our works. The aforementioned James 3:1 is a good example as it suggests that the teachings of those who minister God's Word will be evaluated. Let's consider a couple of other key passages that show that our works will be appraised at the Judgment Seat:

> **If any man builds on this foundation** (of Jesus Christ) **using gold, silver, costly stones, wood, hay or straw, ^{13} his work will be shown for what it is, because the Day will bring it to light. It will be revealed with fire, and the fire will test the quality of each man's work. ^{14} If what he has built survives, he will receive his reward. ^{15} If it is burned up, <u>he will suffer loss</u>; he himself will be saved, but only as one escaping through the flames.**
> **1 Corinthians 3:12-15**

This passage contextually refers to a pastor's work of building a church congregation, that is, a group of Christian disciples (see verses 6-10 for verification). The foundation that the minister builds on is **salvation through Christ**, which is received through **repentance & faith**—the first two basic doctrines of Christianity (Mark 1:15 & Acts 20:21). The pastor can build on this foundation with gold, silver and costly stones or with wood, hay and straw. "Gold, silver and costly stones" is a metaphor for sound biblical doctrine and godly leadership whereas "wood, hay and straw" represent unsound doctrine and ineffective or abusive non-leadership.

At the Judgment Seat every minister's work will be tested by fire. If what they have built survives they will be rewarded. We'll consider these rewards at length in chapter 7. The only works that will survive are those determined to be "gold, silver and costly stones."

If, however, the ministers' works are "wood, hay and straw" they will be burned up. The ministers themselves won't lose their salvation but they will certainly "suffer loss." This indicates that even though it is technically *their works* that will be tested and burned, these ministers will personally experience **the pain of loss** as a result.

What about abusive pastors and teachers who administer "wood, hay and straw" to such a harmful degree that it severely damages people, even driving some away from the Lord—in effect destroying their Christian faith? Paul goes on to answer this:

> **Don't you know that you yourselves are God's temple and that God's Spirit lives in you? ¹⁷ If anyone destroys God's temple, God will destroy him; for God's temple is sacred and you are that temple.**
> **1 Corinthians 3:16-17**

This is a sobering warning for all Christian ministers. Paul makes it clear that every believer is "God's temple"; every Christian is a sacred temple in which the Holy Spirit dwells. Verse 17 solemnly declares that **God will *destroy* any person who destroys this temple**. The context is referring to pastors and teachers who destroy Christians with their "wood, hay and straw," which—again—represent unbiblical doctrine and abusive actions or incompetence. Many have used verse 17 to preach against smoking and alcohol abuse but the context is plainly referring to ministers whose teachings and actions cause people to fall away from the Lord, in effect destroying God's temple.

We all know what Paul's talking about here. Jim Jones is a prime example of a supposed Christian minister whose work ultimately destroyed naïve believers. His work could therefore be categorized as "wood, hay and straw." David Koresh is another fitting example. These are two well-known cases; there are, no doubt, less known examples in your area. Pedophile "priests" are an obvious one.

Notice what verse 17 plainly says the Lord will do to such a (false) minister whose work destroys people: "God will *destroy* him." This means that God will cut the abusive, hypocritical minister off from salvation and cast him into the lake of fire where He will "destroy both soul and body," as Christ put it in Matthew 10:28. Please note that God will *destroy* such persons—**eradicate them from existence**, which includes the horror and torment thereof—not subject them to never-ending roasting torture (Hebrews 10:26-27,31). This is further support for literal everlasting destruction.

Although this passage from 1 Corinthians 3 contextually refers to the testing of the work of pastors and teachers—and any fivefold minister (Ephesians 4:11-13)—we can apply it to *all* Christians because every believer is called to serve the Lord on this earth, even though the majority is not called to pastoral/teaching ministry. Each Christian will have works that God calls him or her to do and these works will be appraised at the Judgment Seat of Christ. For example, God will call Christians to 'witness' to certain people in their lives, which includes nonverbal witnessing, that is, being a "living epistle"; this work will ultimately be tested at the Judgment Seat. Their motives will be evaluated: Did they verbally witness to these people because they love them as God loves them and are following the leading of the Holy Spirit or did they do it to fulfill an evangelistic quota or to appear pious? Needless to say, works produced from fleshly motives are "wood, hay and straw" and will be burned up.

All this explains why James said: "Not many of you should become teachers, my fellow believers, because you know that **we who teach will be judged more strictl**y" (James 3:1). Those who preach and teach God's Word will be held accountable for what they teach at the Judgment Seat of Christ. It goes without saying that if you teach/preach the Word—including posts & memes on the internet—make sure that what you say is as biblical as possible. Defending false teaching on the grounds that your mentor teaches it or your sect supports it won't cut it. Don't be a wimpy "yes man" or "yes woman" to the erroneous doctrines others preach just because it's popular and convenient to do so.

Christ taught a parable that coincides with Paul's teaching from 1 Corinthians 3:

> "**Who then is the faithful and wise manager, who the master puts in charge of his servants to give them their food allowance at the proper time?** [43]**It will be good for that servant who the master finds doing so when he returns.** [44] **I tell you the truth, he will put him in charge of all his possessions.** [45] **But suppose the servant says to himself, 'My master is taking a long time in**

> coming,' and he then begins to beat the menservants and maidservants and to eat and drink and get drunk. ⁴⁶ The master of that servant will come on a day when he does not expect him and at an hour he is not aware of. He will cut him to pieces and assign him a place with the unbelievers."
>
> ⁴⁷ "That servant who knows his master's will and does not get ready or does not do what his master wants will be <u>beaten with many blows</u>. ⁴⁸But the one who does not know and does things deserving punishment will be <u>beaten with few blows</u>. From everyone who has been given much, much will be demanded; and from the one who has been entrusted with much, much more will be asked."
>
> Luke 12:42-48

The "master" in this story is an obvious reference to Jesus Christ. He goes away and puts a "manager" in charge of his "servants" until his return. The "manager" refers to Christian ministers (apostles, pastors, teachers and so on) whom Jesus puts in charge of believers, referred to as "servants." The master (Jesus) instructs the manager (Christian minister) to properly feed and take care of his servants (believers) until his eventual return. One of the primary tasks of ministers is to "feed" the people under their care a proper Scriptural diet so that the believers can mature and learn to walk in newness of life (see 1 Peter 2:2, Ephesians 4:11-15 & Hebrews 5:12-13). In verses 43-44 Jesus says that the minister who does this will be rewarded. He then brings up those ministers who will be penalized for their "wood, hay and straw" in verses 45-48.

Verse 45 shows an abusive minister who damages those under his "care," not to mention indulges in gluttony and drunkenness. Verse

46 solemnly declares that such a minister will be "cut to pieces"—that is, severely flogged—and **cast away as an unbeliever**.

In verses 47-48 Christ says that some "servants" will be beaten with many blows and some with few blows based on their level of spiritual maturity and awareness.[5] The Messiah refers to these people as "servants" and not hypocrites, as was the case with the abusive minister noted in verses 45-46. So Jesus is talking about legitimate Christians who will be judged and penalized at the Judgment Seat. We can confidently conclude this because only believing Christians can be referred to as Christ's "servants," not unbelievers. The abusive minister in verse 45 is initially referred to as a "servant" but is exposed as a "hypocrite," which literally means 'actor.' So we're talking about a person who is only *pretending* to be a servant of Christ. He's a *fake*. This person may have begun as a legitimate Christian servant but somehow became corrupt over time. Position, power, pride, money, lust, etc. can easily corrupt any of us and cause us to fall away from the Lord if we fail to guard our hearts (Proverbs 4:23).

Whether the servant is punished with many blows or few blows, the fact is that this punishment is of a *limited* duration. The words "many" and "few" are not specific, but both indicate a limit to the "blows."

Penalties for Believers at the Judgment Seat vs. Reaping the Wages of Sin for Fakes

We observed earlier that one of the penalties believers might experience at the Bema Judgment will be to "suffer loss" (1

---

[5] The LORD holds people responsible to **the light they have**, as observed in John 9:41, 15:22,24 and James 4:17.

Corinthians 3:15). This is keeping with the biblical example. Consider David, "a man after God's own heart" and arguably Israel's greatest king: He was in contract with the LORD under the Old Covenant and yet he foolishly committed adultery with Bathsheba and indirectly murdered her husband. After Nathan's rebuke David passionately repented (Psalm 51) and the LORD forgave him. As such, he didn't have to suffer death—the official "wages of sin"—***but*** God penalized him with lesser punishments: His infant son died and "the sword would never depart from his house." See 2 Samuel 12:10-14 for verification.

The only "believers" who will reap the wages of sin in the age to come—eternal death—are those who won't be "forgiven... in the age to come," which includes the aforementioned abusive "ministers" exposed as hypocrites, that is, counterfeits. Any individual *not* forgiven by the LORD must reap the wages of sin and that wage is death (Romans 6:23).

Those believers who are "penalized and ultimately forgiven," as put earlier, will obviously be humble & repentant when they stand before the Lord at the Judgment Seat, like David was after Nathan's rebuke. This unlocks God's grace and forgiveness (James 4:6 & 1 Peter 5:5). Even though this is so, the above passages plainly say that they will receive "what is due them" for the "bad," which could be as light as "suffering loss" or as extreme as suffering "many blows." Of course, the latter phrase was used in a parable—a *figurative* story—so we can't say it will be literal blows, but it will be akin to that. It goes without saying that it won't be a fun experience, which explains why Paul said "Since then, we know what it is to fear the Lord."

Such punishment is in keeping with the LORD's general policy regarding people who are in covenant with Him: Penalties for disobedience and rewards for obedience (Deuteronomy 28).

Extreme examples of the latter concerning believers during the age of grace include Ananias & Sapphira (Acts 5:1-10) and "Jezebel" & her followers at the church in Thyatira (Revelation 2:20-23). I realize that it could be argued that these people weren't really believers even though they were functioning as believers within the context of local assemblies. If this is the case then they will be exposed as fakes when they stand before the Lord and suffer damnation, like all unrepentant unbelievers.

But why do some suffer the full penalty of sin—everlasting destruction—and others are simply penalized (suffering "loss" or "blows") and forgiven? It's based on the Lord's just judgment: The former are exposed as actors whom the Lord "never knew" (Matthew 7:15-23) whereas the latter are legitimate members of the body of Christ, despite the folly of their unconfessed sins and dubious quality of some of their works.

Let me share a comparison in the natural world: A Christian guy I know started straying from the Lord over a period of years and ended up foolishly robbing a truck stop of $3500. He said he was hopped-up on pills when he did it. Several hours later and many miles away he "came to his senses" and returned the stolen loot to the store: He put it in a trash can behind the facility and then called the manager, humbly apologized, and told him where the money was located, which they found. While he committed an armed robbery, he ultimately realized his error and humbly repented—proving it by returning the money. Compare this real-life story to a guy who robs a similar store, maybe even kills someone doing it, and is later caught after blowing all the money. The former, my friend, was clearly repentant and the judge took this into account when he was sentenced. Nevertheless, he was judged with a 3-year prison sentence, plus probation. The latter, by contrast, is sternly given the maximum punishment and justly so.

I should add that genuine believers *cannot* reap the wages of sin for unconfessed sin — death — because they're spiritually regenerated of the imperishable seed of Christ (1 Peter 1:23) and therefore intrinsically possess eternal life in their spirits—i.e. the perpetual life of the-age-to-come. The Greek word for 'seed' is sperm in the Greek (see 1 John 3:9 for verification). In short, they're "born of God" and are therefore "children of God" (John 1:12-13). As such, issuing out the wages of sin isn't even an option.

You Won't Often Hear Ministers Teach These Passages

These passages concerning the Judgment Seat of Christ aren't emphasized by a lot of ministers in the modern world. In practice, they essentially cut them out of the New Testament.

A good example are those ministers who teach that believers only receive rewards at the Judgment Seat of Christ and don't have to answer for unconfessed sin, etc. Those who do this basically cut these passages out of the Scriptures. Frankly, they're not being responsibly balanced with God's Word on the topic, likely because of the official stance of their sect or religious tradition. They might be sincere men & women of God, but they're sincerely wrong on this point or, at least, partially wrong.

These sobering passages are in the New Testament as a vital notice to all believers: We're going to stand before the Lord one day so we need to be wise, not foolish, and humbly *keep in repentance* when we miss it. This clears our spiritual arteries from the blockage of unconfessed sin and assures God's grace continually flowing into our lives. We also need to continually take stock of our works—including our motives and attitudes—and make corrections as necessary. As a minister of the Word I can't very well ignore these pertinent passages since I'm going to "be judged more strictly" and I desperately want the Lord's evaluation to end with "Well done good and faithful servant"!

Let me stress: All of a believer's sins that are "under the blood" are forgiven; it's the sins that are not "under the blood" when he/she dies that must be dealt with at the Judgment Seat. This includes sins of omission as well as ministerial abuses, including passive abuses. If we're talking about a genuine believer then the issue of damnation is off the table because Christ was our substitutionary death; i.e. he suffered death in our place. However, this doesn't give believers a license to sin and get away with it, as in "Gee, Jesus died in my place so now I can get away with unrepentant sin—*yee-haw*."

Consider what Paul said to the Roman believers: "You, then, why do you judge your brother or sister? Or why do you treat them with contempt? For we will all stand before God's judgment seat" (Romans 14:10). He's warning *Christians* to not un-righteously judge fellow believers or to treat them with contempt (that is, to ignore them, despise them or look down on them). Why? Because, if they do and don't repent, they'll be accountable for it when they stand before the Lord at the Judgment Seat. Again, if we're talking about truly spiritually regenerated believers then the issue of damnation is off the table, but they'll still have to answer for such sins because they were never dismissed since they were never confessed—i.e. repented of—*before* they physically died. The LORD is the all-righteous, all-just Judge who will issue out penalties and rewards at the Bema Judgment accordingly.

If this material is new to some, it's going to take a while for it to sink in. However, the truth about the Bema Judgment isn't really new because the passages we've covered have always been a part of Holy Scripture since they were originally written via the Holy

Spirit. They're only "new" to people today because whole camps & sects in the body of Christ ignore them or write them off due to their particular religious tradition. Seminary students go to the same schools their pastors went to and so the error is perpetuated.

This comes down to what God's Word honestly teaches based on a thorough, balanced and unbiased (i.e. non-sectarian) study. To discover the truth, *all* of the pertinent passages on a subject must be considered and seriously evaluated. *All* the pieces of the "puzzle" must fit in their proper place. Those who essentially cut out unmistakable passages or write them off because they don't fit their dubious theology are in error and will have to answer for it when they stand before the Lord Christ at His Judgment Seat, which is ironic since they don't even believe this will happen because they think the Judgment Seat is solely about receiving rewards for believers. The truth about the Bema Judgment is a matter of honestly considering all the relevant texts and drawing the obvious conclusions, even if they happen to disagree with someone's religious tradition or what's currently hip with Evangelicals.

Speaking of which, the idea that believers will only receive rewards at the Judgment Seat of Christ is a stronghold belief in Evangelical circles (amongst others), but the numerous passages we've looked at show differently: Believers will be judged for how they lived their lives and will receive what is "due" them for what they did while in the body—whether good or bad. Unconfessed sins must be addressed and our works will be appraised.

Concluding Words on the Judgment Seat

As noted earlier, 2 Samuel 11-12 shows that David **suffered loss** for his adultery with Bathsheba and murder of Uriah; and 1

Corinthians 3:15 describes penalties at the Judgment Seat in terms of "suffering loss." Verses 16-17 reveal what happens to those who are exposed as fakes, aka hypocrites (Matthew 7:15-23). They will be destroyed, like all unbelievers.

Jesus himself described the penalties for the saved in terms of **being beaten with many or few blows** (Luke 12:47-48). Whether many blows or few, the punishment is of limited duration.

So **suffering loss** and **being justifiably beaten** are the Scriptural descriptions of penalties for believers at the Judgment Seat. Just keep in mind that being beaten with few or many blows is figurative language. In other words, believers will experience a penalty *akin to* a servant in the 1st century being justly beaten, but not abused.

I'm assuming that any such penalties will be addressed *before* rewards, but it's clear that the former will negatively affect the latter, at least as far as "suffering loss" goes. For instance, Christ describes eternal rewards in terms of being placed in authority positions in two parables—Matthew 25:14-30 & Luke 19:15-19. These positions of authority are phrased as being "put in charge of many *things*" in Matthew and "taking charge of many *cities*" in Luke, both of which apply to the eternal age of the new heavens and new earth (2 Peter 3:13 & Revelation 21:1-5). We will examine this next chapter.

I find this biblical data fascinating because, again, you'll rarely hear ministers teach on penalties at the Bema Judgment, which is understandable since people naturally want to hear about eternal rewards, not drawbacks. Yet these kinds of passages are good seeing as how they encourage believers to "keep in repentance" (Matthew & Luke 3:8) and lead holy lives consecrated unto the LORD. The good thing about honestly keeping 'fessed up (1 John

1:8-9) is that God *forgives* the offenses in **this age** so we don't have to answer for them in **the age-to-come**. It's why we are encouraged to wisely "examine" or "test" ourselves (2 Corinthians 13:5), which should be done on a regular basis. I want to hear "Well done good and faithful servant" and not "Dirk, I'm happy you have eternal life, but there are some issues we need to talk about."

The Sheep and Goat Judgment

This particular judgment concerns non-Christians still alive on earth *after* God's judgment falls on humanity during the seven-year Tribulation, which is detailed in Revelation 6-19. When the mighty Christ returns to earth to set up His millennial kingdom He will judge the living nations, as shown in Matthew 25:31-46. They will be judged according to how they treated Tribulation saints, that is, people who embrace the gospel during the Tribulation. You see, believers will be greatly persecuted during the antichrist's worldwide reign of terror. When Christ returns the surviving people of the nations will be judged according to how they treated these Tribulation saints. Those who had regard for believers—that is, the body of Christ on earth—and acted accordingly will be designated as "sheep." They will be spiritually regenerated and allowed to enter the Millennium as born-again mortals. However, those who disregard and persecute believers will be cast into the lake of fire, God's garbage dump, to suffer the second death.

The Sheep and Goat Judgment naturally spurs questions because the Lord does not judge the people subject to this judgment based on faith in response to the gospel of Christ but rather by their good works—specifically, how they treated Christians during the Tribulation. Did they feed them? Give them something to drink? Show them hospitality? Clothe them? Assist them when they were sick? Visit them in prison? Those who did will be blessed with spiritual rebirth & eternal life—just like people in our era who receive the gospel. Those who don't will be condemned to the lake of fire and the corresponding eternal punishment (not eternal punish*ing*; there's a difference).

When I was in my 20s I remember asking a subordinate pastor at the assembly I was attending specific questions about this particular judgment and he just wrote them off with the conclusion that "we can't get dogmatic about it." I found this non-answer unsatisfying and lost a little respect for the man. He clearly didn't have answers so he should've just been honest and admitted it rather than writing off Jesus' elaboration on the Sheep and Goat Judgment as irrelevant, wholly dismissing my questions in the process.

The passage is a fairly long one and it was given by Jesus Christ, the Living Word who is **the truth** (John 14:6). As such, this curious judgment fits *somewhere* in the puzzle of end time events. It's not something to write off on the grounds that "we can't get dogmatic about it," whatever that means. Let's read the passage:

> [31] "<u>When the Son of Man comes in his glory</u>, and all the angels with him, he will sit on his glorious throne. [32] <u>All the nations will be gathered before him</u>, and he will separate the people one from another as a shepherd separates the sheep from the goats. [33] He will put the sheep on his right and the goats on his left.
> [34] "Then the King will say to those on his right, 'Come, you who are blessed by my Father; take your inheritance, the kingdom prepared for you since the creation of the world. [35] For I was hungry and you gave <u>me</u> something to eat, I was

thirsty and you gave <u>me</u> something to drink, I was a stranger and you invited <u>me</u> in, [36] I needed clothes and you clothed <u>me</u>, I was sick and you looked after <u>me</u>, I was in prison and you came to visit <u>me</u>.'

[37] "Then the righteous will answer him, 'Lord, when did we see you hungry and feed you, or thirsty and give you something to drink? [38] When did we see you a stranger and invite you in, or needing clothes and clothe you? [39] When did we see you sick or in prison and go to visit you?'

[40] "The King will reply, 'Truly I tell you, whatever you did for one of the least of these <u>brothers and sisters of mine</u>, you did for <u>me</u>.'

[41] "Then he will say to those on his left, '<u>Depart from me, you who are cursed, into the eternal fire prepared for the devil and his angels</u>. [42] For I was hungry and you gave <u>me</u> nothing to eat, I was thirsty and you gave <u>me</u> nothing to drink, [43] I was a stranger and you did not invite <u>me</u> in, I needed clothes and you did not clothe <u>me</u>, I was sick and in prison and you did not look after <u>me</u>.'

[44] "They also will answer, 'Lord, when did we see you hungry or thirsty or a stranger or needing clothes or sick or in prison, and did not help you?'

[45] "He will reply, 'Truly I tell you, whatever you did not do for one of the least of these, you did not do for <u>me</u>.'

[46] "<u>Then they will go away to eternal punishment, but the righteous to eternal life</u>."

Matthew 25:31-46

The very beginning of this prophecy shows that this "Sheep and Goat Judgment" takes place *after* **Christ's return at the end of the Tribulation and** *before* **the Millennium**. At this time Jesus will judge the living nations—that is, the people around the globe who survived the Great Tribulation. This explains why the Sheep and Goat Judgment is also known as the Judgment of Living Nations or the Pre-Millennial Judgment of Christ. It's important to understand the timing & place of this judgment because this reveals its **context** and "Context is King," a hermeneutical rule.

With this understanding, the Sheep and Goat Judgment is *not* **the Great White Throne Judgment** where dead unregenerated people are resurrected from Sheol (Hades) to be judged (Revelation 20:11-15). Nor does it refer to **the Judgment Seat of Christ**, which is for *believers* or anyone who was in the Church at some point (2 Corinthians 5:10-11).

It's important to point this out because people have been known to remove the Sheep and Goat Judgment from its context and **misapply it** to a wholly different judgment, which naturally results in false doctrine.

It's also important to point out that Jesus' elaboration on the Sheep and Goat Judgment is not a parable. I stress this because some ministers say it's a parable, a symbolic story, on the grounds that Christ's other two teachings from Matthew 25 are parables—The Parable of the Ten Virgins and The Parable of the Bags of Gold. While those are indeed parables it doesn't make his commentary on the Sheep and Goat Judgment a parable. Rather, it's a **prophetic teaching**. This can be seen in Jesus' opening words: "***When*** the Son of Man comes in his glory, and all the angels with him, he will sit on his glorious throne. **All the nations will be gathered before him**, and he will separate the people one from another as a shepherd separates the sheep from the goats." You see? This is **a prophecy of a future event** that will take place when Christ returns to the Earth and judges survivors of the Great Tribulation from all nations. Keep in mind that Jesus is "the Prophet" whom the Israelites were expecting since the time of Moses (Deuteronomy 18:15,18).

I should add that the Lord will judge the people at the Sheep and Goat Judgment **as individuals**, one nation at a time. I say this because each person is responsible for his or her own sin or obedience (see Ezekiel 18).

Proof that the Sheep and Goat Judgment Applies to Living <u>Non-Christians</u> at the End of the Tribulation

Revelation 20:4-6 speaks of the third stage of the resurrection of the righteous, which is called "the first resurrection." This stage of the first resurrection takes place around the same time as the Sheep and Goat Judgment. This was covered in the previous chapter but, to refresh your memory, here's a diagram explaining the three stages of the Resurrection of the Righteous; as well as the Resurrection of the Unrighteous:

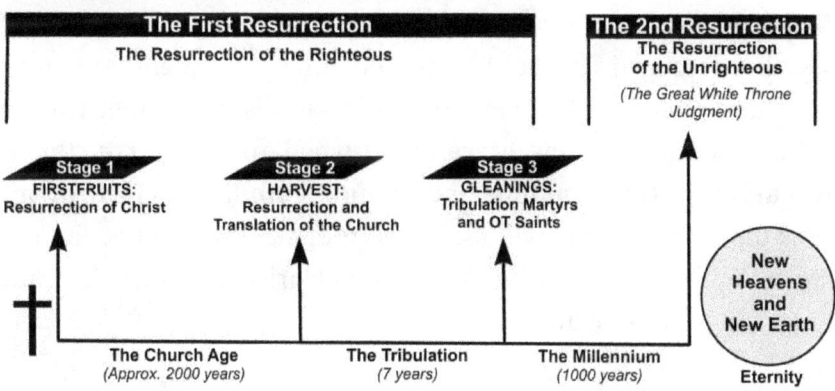

The third stage of this resurrection is detailed in Revelation 20:4-6 and will be similar to the second stage, which takes place at the time of the Rapture: Living believers will receive their resurrection bodies and believers who physically died during the Tribulation (noted in Revelation 6:9-11 and 7:9-15) will receive their glorified bodies. The previous chapter provides details on these things.

I point this out to show that those judged at the Sheep and Goat Judgment are *not* born-again believers, but rather the people of the world—***non-Christians***—who survived the Tribulation after Christ wipes out the Antichrist's army with a mere word (Revelation 19:21). We'll consider additional support momentarily.

What is the Sheep and Goat Judgment All About?

This judgment is all about judging these living, unsaved people to determine who will suffer immediate damnation and who will receive eternal life and be allowed to enter into the Millennium as mortals, yet born-again spiritually, just like genuine believers in our era *have* eternal life while still physically mortal (John 3:36 & 1 John 5:11-12) and are promised a future resurrection with immortal, glorified bodies (1 Corinthians 15:42-44).

All those judged at the Sheep and Goat Judgment are non-Christians. Yet it will be certain to them at this juncture that Jesus *is* Lord because **he has literally returned to the Earth, taken authority of the situation** and **is now standing before them**. Thus the criteria Christ will use at this judgment will *not* be faith in Christ. Why? Because they *all believe* in Christ now since the Lord is right in front of them.

(Keep in mind that the gospel will be preached during the Tribulation via the 144,000 Hebrew evangelists and their converts, not to mention an angel, as Revelation 14:6 shows).

So how does the Lord judge them? Those designated "sheep" will receive eternal life via spiritual rebirth (just like us today) and will be allowed to enter the Millennium—as mortals—**because they assisted persecuted/needy *believers* during the Tribulation**, which will include the aforementioned 144,000 and their millions of converts.

Genuine Christians during the Tribulation will not be part of the one-world Babylonian system and will therefore face hunger, thirst, outcast status, unjust imprisonment and need for clothes/shelter. Christ will judge the living nations as to how they treated *him*—**his body, the Body of Christ**—during the Tribulation. This is in line with the "cup of cold water" principle:

> **"And if anyone gives even a cup of cold water to one of these little ones who is my disciple, truly I tell you, that person will certainly not lose their reward."**
>
> **Matthew 10:42**

Jesus says concerning the Sheep and Goat Judgment: "Truly I tell you, whatever **you** [non-Christians] did for one of the least of these **brothers and sisters of mine** [Christians], you did for **me**" (verse 40). This reveals that he's talking about how these people treated **the body of Christ** during the Tribulation. This is similar to what Jesus said to Paul when unbelieving Saul persecuted the Church:

> **Meanwhile, Saul was still breathing out murderous threats against the Lord's disciples. He went to the high priest [2] and asked him for**

> letters to the synagogues in Damascus, so that if he found any there who belonged to the Way (i.e. Christianity), whether men or women, he might take them as prisoners to Jerusalem. ³ **As he neared Damascus on his journey, suddenly a light from heaven flashed around him. ⁴ He fell to the ground and heard a voice say to him, "Saul, Saul, why do you persecute <u>me</u>?"**
> ⁵ **"Who are you, Lord?" Saul asked.**
> **"<u>I am Jesus</u>, <u>whom you are persecuting</u>," he replied.**
>
> Acts 9:1-5

This shows beyond any shadow of doubt that the "living nations" whom the Lord judges at the Sheep and Goat Judgment are all unsaved **non-Christians**. I say "living" nations because Jesus says nothing about resurrecting the dead from Sheol (Hades) at this judgment, as will be done at the Great White Throne Judgment a thousand years later. And, furthermore, Matthew 25:31-32 specifically says: "**When the Son of Man comes in his glory**, and all the angels with him, he will sit on his glorious throne. **All the nations will be gathered before him**." This is referring to people of all nations still alive at Christ's Second Coming. Again, this is **the context**.

This answers a point a minister made about this judgment:

> *Jesus won't be saying to the sheep on His right, "Enter into the kingdom prepared for you from the foundation of the world, because your doctrinal positions were spot on."*

What this brother says is true because the people Christ evaluates at this judgment aren't even Christians to begin with; so it's unlikely that they would know much, if any, biblical Christian doctrine, let alone be held accountable for it. The Lord will judge these people solely based on how they treated Christ's "brothers and sisters" during the Tribulation, which—again—is in line with the "cup of cold water" principle of Matthew 10:42.

As for judging people for their doctrinal positions, this will happen to *Christians* at the Judgment Seat of Christ. James 3:1 says point blank that those who teach God's Word will be "judged more strictly," which shows that they *will* be judged according to the true or false doctrines they spread. This will even include internet posts, memes, etc. *Whoever* teaches from the Scriptures will be judged for it and rewarded or penalized accordingly, depending on if what they conveyed was true or false or (in some cases) somewhere in between.

While you can certainly teach important principles from the Sheep and Goat Judgment, like how the Lord wants us to meet the immediate needs of suffering saints and people in general, **this judgment is only applicable to the *un*regenerated living nations at the time of Christ's Second Coming to the Earth**. To take the Sheep and Goat Judgment and apply it to the Judgment Seat of Christ is a case of misapplying a passage. It's not even applicable to the Great White Throne Judgment because that judgment comprises resurrected unsaved people from throughout history and about half of them would never have even met a Christian, which means it would be impossible for Christ to judge them based on how they treated Christ's "brothers and sisters" or anyone else in covenant with God, like Old Testament saints.

We'll get back to the Sheep and Goat Judgment shortly. It's necessary at this point to briefly touch on some related issues…

The Salvation Equation

While genuine believers' works will be evaluated at the Judgment Seat of Christ they're not saved by their works. As Paul declared: "at the present time there is a remnant chosen by grace. And **if by grace, then it cannot be based on works**; if it were, grace would no longer be grace" (Romans 11:5-6) and, of course, Ephesians 2:8-9: "For **it is by grace you have been saved, through faith**—and this is not from yourselves, it is the gift of God—**not by works, so that no one can boast.**"

We are saved by grace—God's graciousness—*through* faith and **not** by works (deeds). This is a foundational truth and it's absolutely imperative to grasp it, but some people have gotten off-balanced and misinterpreted it to mean that works/deeds are next to meaningless when nothing could be further from the truth. ***True faith always produces works*** and this is obviously what James meant in his epistle in light of the clarity of the above passages:

> **You see that a person is considered righteous <u>by what they do</u> and <u>not by faith alone</u>...** [26] **As the body without the spirit is dead, so <u>faith without deeds is dead</u>.**
> **James 2:24,26**

With this data in mind, if we were to come up with a biblical **equation** to correspond to salvation in Christ (like 2 + 2 = 4) how would we phrase it? Here it is:

True Faith = Salvation (+ Fruit + Works)

This equation indicates that **genuine faith** *results in* eternal salvation, as well as fruit of the spirit & the corresponding works.

Simply put, you're not saved by works; you're saved by faith; and true faith will produce fruit, which—in turn—produces works (deeds).

We already know by the above passages that faith naturally results in works or deeds. So let me explain why 'fruit' is included in the equation and how it ties into our topic.

Genuine faith will naturally produce the fruit of the spirit (Galatians 5:19-23) as the believer learns to put off the old self and live according to his/her new nature with the help of the Holy Spirit (Ephesians 4:22-24). Such believers will automatically start to produce the various **fruits of the spirit**, including love, kindness and goodness. This, in turn, results in **good works**, which means deeds or actions, if you look up the Greek word.

Here are a couple examples: I love some brothers who are in prison and so I sacrifice the time in order to write, phone & visit them periodically; or you may buy a sister a new pair of glasses because she lacks the funds. Such good works spring from the fruit we're already bearing because we're spirit-controlled and not flesh-ruled. This explains Paul's prayer for the Colossian believers to "bear **fruit** in every **good work**" (Colossians 1:10), which shows that **it's possible to do a work *without* bearing fruit of the spirit**. Meaning: We can do good works in the flesh, that is, produce good works while controlled by the sinful nature. Quasi-Christian religionists (like Mormons & Jehovah's False Witnesses), Muslims and Sciencefictionologists do this all the time. This explains Paul's observation in the love chapter: "If I give all I possess to the poor and give over my body to hardship **that I may boast**, but **do not have love**, I gain nothing" (1 Corinthians 13:3).

This all ties into something Christ taught:

¹⁵ "Watch out for <u>false prophets</u>. They come to you in sheep's clothing, but inwardly they are ferocious wolves. ¹⁶ <u>By their fruit you will recognize them</u>. Do people pick grapes from thornbushes, or figs from thistles? ¹⁷ Likewise, every good tree bears good fruit, but a bad tree bears bad fruit. ¹⁸ A good tree cannot bear bad fruit, and a bad tree cannot bear good fruit. ¹⁹Every tree that does not bear good fruit is cut down and thrown into the fire. ²⁰ Thus, <u>by their fruit you will recognize them</u>.

²¹ "<u>Not everyone who says to me, 'Lord, Lord,' will enter the kingdom of heaven</u>, <u>but only the one who does the will of my Father who is in heaven</u>. ²² <u>Many</u> will say to me on that day, '<u>Lord, Lord, did we not prophesy in your name and in your name drive out demons and in your name perform many miracles</u>?' ²³ Then I will tell them plainly, '<u>I never knew you. Away from me, you evildoers!</u>' "

Matthew 7:15-23

As you can see, the Messiah said we can recognize false ministers by **their fruit or lack thereof**. These religionists who come before Jesus to be judged are proud of their good works and, incredibly, boast of them (it's what proud religionists do). But the Lord says he never knew them **because** they were "evildoers" (i.e. "workers of iniquity"). Since Christ does not dispute their good works—prophesying, exorcising demons and performing miracles—we can assume that they really performed these religious deeds. The problem is that they were "evildoers" who practiced iniquity, which shows they were flesh-ruled with no care to "keep in repentance" (Matthew & Luke 3:8). In other words, their regular sinful actions testified against them despite their good works.

We're talking about people like the Pharisees who regularly performed good works (mostly as a show to convince themselves and others how "godly" they supposedly were) while unrepentantly living in the flesh in secret.

The "Sheep" Who Are Allowed to Enter the Millennium

Let's get back to the Sheep and Goat Judgment and the "sheep" who are allowed to enter the Millennium as born-again believers: These mortals will breed throughout the thousand years all over the world. Despite the completely righteous government of Christ, many of their descendants will be susceptible to the devil's deception when he's released from the Abyss at the end of the Millennium to "deceive the nations in the four corners of the earth" (Revelation 20:7-8). Satan coerces them through deception to, amazingly, attack Christ and his righteous government in Jerusalem. These deceived **descendants of** the original "sheep" illustrate that they're not truly believers and therefore not spiritually regenerated (even if they genuinely were at one point), just like there are confessing Christians in our midst who just go through the motions but aren't actually born of Christ's seed (1 Peter 1:23 & 1 John 3:9). Thankfully, this won't be the case in the eternal age-to-come because there won't be any mortals with ungodly natures. (We'll examine the nature of eternal life next chapter).

While life during the Millennium will be a veritable utopia compared to our current age because of **1.** the righteous government of Christ and **2.** the absence of the devil & his filthy spirits to deceive people, there will still be sin because these mortals will yet have sinful natures, which explains why many of them will be open prey to Satan's deceptions when he's released from the Abyss at the end of the thousand years. There will also be aging, pain and death despite the return of longer lifespans. Not to mention the earth and universe will yet be burdened by the bondage to decay, which is entropy.

"Produce FRUIT in keeping with repentance"

The Greek for 'fruit' in Matthew 7:15-23 (quoted above) is the same word for 'fruit' in Galatians 5:22-23—*karpos*—and so refers to **the fruit of the spirit**, which of course includes holiness (as there are more than just nine fruits of the spirit and Ephesians 4:24 shows that holiness is one of 'em). You could even make the argument that holiness is the whole of the fruits of the spirit, indicating that the believer is spirit-controlled with the help of the Holy Spirit rather than flesh-ruled.

The "false prophets" Jesus references in Matthew 7:15-23 obviously weren't naïve young believers, but rather seasoned people who proposed to speak for God in their "ministry" on earth. Yet Christ condemns them. Despite their great religious works and their corresponding boasting, they will be damned. **This passage shows that good works by themselves won't save people**.

While I suppose it could be argued that they were unbelievers all along, it's more likely that they started out sincere, but were corrupted at some point, which is possible in light of clear passages like Galatians 5:21, Hebrews 10:26-27 and 2 Peter 2:20-21.

This, of course, begs the question: How long can a genuine believer walk in known sin without care of repentance before the Lord cuts him/her out of the kingdom? The Parable of the Barren Fig Tree offers some insight:

"But <u>unless you repent</u>, you too will all <u>perish</u>."
⁶ Then he told this parable: "A man had a fig tree growing in his vineyard, and he went to look for <u>fruit</u> on it but did not find any. ⁷ So he said to the man who took care of the vineyard, 'For three years now I've been coming to look for <u>fruit</u> on this fig tree and haven't found any. Cut it down! Why should it use up the soil?'
⁸ " 'Sir,' the man replied, 'leave it alone for one more year, and I'll dig around it and fertilize it. ⁹If it bears <u>fruit</u> next year, fine! If not, then <u>cut it down</u>.' "

Luke 13:5-9

The symbolism in the parable is obvious: The owner of the vineyard represents God, the fruitless fig tree represents an individual in covenant with God who's not bearing fruit, and the caretaker represents Jesus, the mediator between the owner and the fig tree. The owner (God) wants to cut the fig tree down because **it hasn't produced fruit in *three years***, but the caretaker (Jesus) intercedes and convinces the owner to give the tree *one more year* wherein the caretaker will do everything he can to get it to be fruitful. If the tree still hasn't produced fruit by the end of the fourth year the owner and caretaker agree to cut it down and remove it from the vineyard. 'Fruit,' by the way, is the same Greek word *karpos (kar-POS)* noted above.

What we see in this story is patience, mercy and grace: The owner of the vineyard and the caretaker—who represent the heavenly Father and Christ—are willing to give the tree a total of *four years* to be fruitful before ultimately removing it from the vineyard, *if* they must. The story is figurative so we can't take it strictly literal, i.e. that God will pluck someone out of the kingdom if they're fruitless for exactly four years. What we *can* get from it, however, is that God's patience, mercy and grace are awesome and He will do everything He can to get us to be fruitful. He's invested in us greatly and understandably wants us to be productive. Another thing we can get from the parable is that when the Lord's mercy ends His judgment begins and he'll cut off when/if necessary.

The New Testament instructs us to "produce fruit in keeping with repentance" (see Matthew & Luke 3:8 where 'fruit' is the same Greek word *karpos*). We produce fruit, of course, by walking in the spirit—being spirit-controlled rather than flesh-ruled. The book of Ephesians calls this "walking as children of the light" and adds "for the fruit of the light consists in all goodness and righteousness and truth" (Ephesians 5:8-9).

Obviously **there's a link between producing fruit and keeping with repentance**: Believers who fail to "keep with repentance" are less likely to produce fruit since they're obviously more flesh-ruled than spirit-controlled. Only when believers genuinely repent after being convicted will God forgive them of the sin in question and cleanse them from all unrighteousness (1 John 1:8-9). This is walking in God's grace (favor). Those who stubbornly resist repenting, however, harden their hearts. The more they do this the harder their hearts become. The book of Hebrews describes this as "sin's deceitfulness" (Hebrews 3:8,12-13). It can get to the point where they stop producing fruit to God altogether because they're in a state of non-grace due to the build-up of sin which *isn't* forgiven and therefore they're *not* purged of the corresponding unrighteousness. When believers backslide into this hardhearted, fruitless mode the Parable of the Barren Fig Tree applies: After a generous "grace period" these fruitless, unrepentant 'believers' will be cut out of the kingdom, just like the fruitless fig tree is rooted out of the vineyard. Such people would include the false ministers addressed in Matthew 7:15-23, detailed above.

Speaking of that passage, it's likely a reference to the Judgment Seat of Christ, which is where members of the Church will stand before the Lord and give an account. This will presumably include those who *were* members of the Church at some point.

The basis for eternal salvation at the Judgment Seat is not good works; if it were, the believing thief on the cross *wouldn't* be saved. It all comes down to whether a person is **in Christ** or not **in Christ**—that is, *in* the kingdom or not. This explains The Parable of the Wedding Banquet from Matthew 22 where the person without "wedding clothes" is rejected and condemned, like the fruitless "prophets" of Matthew 7:15-23. Christians are either "clothed with Christ" or not. Those who *aren't* are in for a rude awakening when they stand before the Lord because they're no longer even believers, as far as God is concerned. They've been "rooted from the vineyard." While good works and the motive for them will be evaluated at the Judgment Seat, and believers will be rewarded or penalized accordingly, their good works *don't* determine their salvation.

Another Example of Misapplying the Sheep and Goat Judgment

As already covered, James statement in James 2:24 was later clarified by Paul—clearly the greater apostle—in Romans 11:5-6, Ephesians 2:8-9 and Colossians 1:10. Scripture interprets Scripture; and nowhere in the epistles do we see good works being the criteria for salvation. For instance, when Paul encourages believers to "*excel* in the grace of giving" he *doesn't* add "because, if you don't, you're a wicked goat condemned to the lake of fire!" (2 Corinthians 8:7). In the same context of giving to needy believers he says "Whoever sows sparingly will also reap sparingly, and whoever sows generously will also reap generously"

(2 Corinthians 9:6). Once again, he doesn't link donating money to damnation or salvation. While giving to the poor is important and obviously a focal point of some ministries it's not the all-and-end-all of Christianity.

In the same context Paul says "Each of you should give **what you have decided in your heart to give**, not reluctantly or under compulsion, for God loves a cheerful giver" (2 Corinthians 9:7). The LORD only wants believers to give **out of a giving heart that's happy to give**; he doesn't want believers to give reluctantly or under compulsion—which includes being coerced by ministers preaching condo. There's no condo in Paul's request for funds for needy Christians in this section of Scripture (2 Corinthians 8-9). He shares the need, encourages the Corinthians to give, stresses that they'll be rewarded, and then adds that they should only give what they *decide* to *gladly* give. This is the only way they'll be blessed for their giving; otherwise they'd be giving from the flesh to earn salvation or whatever, which is what Hindus, Muslims, et al. do.

Another thing we can get from this passage is that Paul didn't view believers as pawns to fund ministry projects which he considered important, including altruistic ones. He respected and loved the believers where they were spiritually and permitted them to make up their own minds as led of the Spirit (or not led of the Spirit).

I bring this up because I've heard the Sheep and Goat Judgment misapplied by some ministers for the purpose of manipulating believers into giving money for their altruistic ministry projects. These projects may be wonderful, but it doesn't condone the practice of using condo by misapplying a passage in order to twist believers' arms into donating money.

Of course it's true that faith without deeds is dead, which would mean that the believer who lacks good works also lacks fruit of the spirit since **authentic good works are always a natural extension of the fruit of the spirit and therefore any *other* good work is a dead work because it stems from the flesh**. But, I should stress, a fruitless believer isn't kicked out of the kingdom immediately; he/she is given a gracious time period to produce fruit because God is merciful & patient and greatly desires for them to be productive, as the Parable of the Barren Fig Tree illustrates.

The fact that good works are not the basis for salvation for believers at the Judgment Seat of Christ is further proof that the people judged at the Sheep and Goat Judgment are all unsaved because they are all judged by their works.

Unbelievers aren't judged according to the gospel because they never *received* it; as such, God judges them "according to what they had done as recorded in the books" where "their consciences (will) bear witness, and their thoughts will either accuse or excuse them" (Roman 2:12-16 & Revelation 20:11-15). "What they had done" would include rejecting (or, at least, ignoring) the message of Christ for those of whom this applies.

The False Prophets of Matthew 7:15-23 and the Judgment Seat of Christ

As stated earlier, it's likely that Matthew 7:15-23 is a depiction of the Judgment Seat of Christ even though the Lord rejects the false ministers. How so? These people **confess Jesus as Lord** and illustrate that they performed great works, like prophesying, exorcizing demons and miracles, which implies that they functioned within Church circles. The Lord doesn't deny that they did these good works, but condemns them. The implication is that these confessing "Christians" are shocked by the Messiah's rejection. We can therefore assume that the Judgment Seat is for anyone who confesses Jesus as Lord or were in the kingdom at some point. With this understanding, notice that Jesus doesn't judge them by their good works **because they had good works**; instead he judges them by their fruit or lack thereof, which indicates that they were flesh-ruled "evildoers" despite their good works! **This is in contrast to the Sheep and Goat Judgment where Christ judges the people solely on the basis of their good works**; and, more specifically, by how they treated persecuted believers during the Tribulation.

The Judgment of Old Testament Saints

The sixth basic doctrine of eternal judgment also applies to the judgment of Old Testament saints. These people will be judged at the time of their resurrection when the Lord returns to the earth to establish His millennial reign, which takes place at the end of the Tribulation, as shown in the following two passages:

> **"At that time Michael, the great prince who protects your people, will arise. There will be a time of distress such as has not happened from the beginning of nations until then. But at that time your people—everyone whose name is found written in the book—will be delivered. ²Multitudes who sleep in the dust of the earth will awake: some to everlasting life, others to shame and everlasting contempt."**
> **Daniel 12:1-2**

Daniel prophesies that the resurrection of the Israelites will not take place until after a "time of distress" so great that such a thing never occurred before in the history of humanity. This refers to the Tribulation detailed in the book of Revelation (chapters 6-19). Daniel speaks in general terms of the righteous who will be delivered or resurrected at this time. He refers to them as "your people"—i.e. God's people—and "everyone whose name is found written in the book," which would of course include more than just Old Testament holy people; it would include Christian martyrs during the Tribulation, as well as living believers who survived the Tribulation.

The Lord gets more specific about the resurrection and judgment of Old Testament saints in this passage:

> **Jesus said to them, "Truly I tell you, at the renewal of all things, when the Son of Man sits on his glorious throne, you who have followed me will also sit on twelve thrones, judging the twelve tribes of Israel. [29] And everyone who has left houses or brothers or sisters or father or mother or wife or children or fields for my sake will receive a hundred times as much and will inherit eternal life. [30] But many who are first will be last, and many who are last will be first."**
>
> **Matthew 19:28-30**

Some might inquire why Old Testament saints are not resurrected at the time of Jesus' return for his Church—that is, the Rapture—which is when believers are either bodily resurrected or translated (1 Thessalonians 4:13-18), but this idea is negated by the obvious fact that the Rapture concerns the Lord's return for his Church—his bride—and not his return for people of the Old Testament period who were in covenant with God.

7

ETERNAL LIFE

It's only fitting that we end this book with the wonderful gift of eternal life, especially since we addressed some pretty sobering issues last chapter.

Understanding the nature of eternal life would fall under the sixth basic doctrine—eternal judgment—because God's judgment of any individual who's *in Christ* is to grant them the gift of eternal life, which is the main benefit of the gospel, along with the corresponding reconciliation with God and forgiveness of sins.

What we want to focus on in this chapter is the nature of eternal life as far as eternity goes. I'm talking about what it will be like in the eternal age of **the new heavens and new earth**, traditionally referred to as "heaven" since the time of Augustine.

A New Earth and Universe

The Bible teaches that time—as we know it—will culminate with "a new heaven and new earth" wherein there will be "no more death or mourning or crying or pain, for the old order of things has passed away" (Revelation 21:1-4). This "new heaven" refers to the physical universe and not to what is commonly understood as 'heaven,' that is, the spiritual dimension where God dwells. You see, the sky and universe are often referred to as "heaven" or "the heavens" in the Bible; for example, Psalm 19:1 states: "The **heavens** declare the glory of God; **the skies** proclaim the work of his hands." This is an example of Hebrew poetry known as synonymous parallelism wherein the second part of the verse simply repeats the first part in different words. In this case, "the heavens" in the first part is confirmed as "the skies" in the second. The context of the passage determines the proper definition, which is the hermeneutical rule "context is king."[6]

God's heaven—which is referred to as "the *third* heaven" in Scripture (2 Corinthians 12:2)—is perfect and has no reason to be made new. It's the earth and the physical universe that will be made new—"new" in the sense that the maladies of evil, death, pain, disease and decay will be forever eradicated. As declared in Romans 8:21: "the creation itself [the earth & universe and all living things] will be *liberated* from its bondage to decay and brought into the glorious *freedom* of the children of God." The LORD's goal is to ultimately *liberate* humanity from our miserable confinement to pain, decay and death, not to mention evil itself. This includes our **environment**—the earth & universe.

Will We "Spend Eternity in Heaven"?

We've all heard it said that the redeemed will "spend eternity in heaven." Whether this is true or not depends on your definition of heaven. If 'heaven' refers *exclusively* to the spiritual dimension where God's throne is located—that is, the celestial realm that

---

[6] See the article on hermeneutics at the Fountain of Life site.

gave birth to our physical universe (Hebrews 11:3)—then the answer is no, we will not spend eternity in heaven. If, on the other hand, 'heaven' refers to what the Bible calls "the new heavens and new earth, the home of righteousness" (2 Peter 3:13) then, yes, we will spend eternity in heaven.

However, since **the phrase "spend eternity in heaven" is *not* found anywhere in Scripture**, I think it's important to stick to actual biblical expressions when discussing eternal life so there's no misunderstanding. After all, it's *the truth* that will set us free, not clichéd religious sayings.

This is especially important when you consider the fact that when 99.9% of people hear the term 'heaven' they automatically think of the blissful ethereal realm where angels dwell; and understandably so since this is its primary definition. As such, when people hear the phrase "spend eternity in heaven" they naturally think of living on a cloud playing a harp forever. There are two problems with this: **1.** It's not true and the problem with false beliefs is that they can't set people free; only the truth can set us free. **2.** Since error is incapable of setting us free it's incapable of giving us life. In other words, the truth will always excite and inspire the spiritual individual, whereas falsities do the precise opposite—they won't inspire us or excite us; in fact, they'll bore us, limit us or ruin us in one way or another. Why? Because truth equals life and freedom whereas error equals death and bondage. Consider, for example, the conventional imagery of eternal life—hanging out on a cloud playing a harp forever. Although this would surely be fun for a few days or perhaps even weeks, we're talking about *eternity* here— forever and ever. Is this all we have to look forward to? If so, no wonder so few Christians are excited about the notion of eternal life. They find it *boring,* not to mention fantastical.

The plain truth of God's Word, by contrast, is exhilarating and fascinating. Consider this example…

The New Jerusalem will come "Down out of Heaven from God"

We've all heard about the gates of heaven referred to as "the pearly gates," yet in the Bible this is actually a description of the twelve gates of the new Jerusalem, a very large city that is presently in the spiritual realm of God, i.e. heaven (Revelation 21:21). Guess what ultimately happens to this city? After God renovates the earth & universe, the New Jerusalem will come "down *out of heaven* from God." This is clearly stated *three times* in Scripture: Revelation 3:12 and 21:2 & 21:10. My point is that this awesome city will not stay in heaven; it will come down "out of heaven" to rest on the new earth. Who knows? It may even be able to hover over the planet and more, like traverse the galaxies; after all, it's going to travel from heaven to earth *intact*.

This city, the new earth and the entire new universe will be the eternal home of all those who partake of God's gift of eternal life. Note for yourself:

> **"Blessed are the meek**
> **for they will inherit the Earth."**
> **Matthew 5:5**
>
> **The righteous will inherit the land** [i.e. the earth]
> **and dwell in it forever.**
> **Psalm 37:29**

We see here that the "meek" and the "righteous" will inherit the *earth* and dwell in it *forever*. This would naturally include the physical universe in which the earth resides (more on this momentarily). My point is that humanity will inherit the new earth & universe as its **eternal home**. Notice what the Bible plainly states in this regard:

> **The highest heavens belong to the LORD,**
> **but the earth he has given to man.**
> **Psalm 115:16**

"The highest heavens" belong to God. This refers to the highest spiritual realm where God's throne is located, which, as previously noted, is called "the third heaven" in Scripture. Although, believers are indeed "seated… in the heavenly realms" in Christ in a *positional* sense (Ephesians 2:6), humankind will *not* inherit this highest heavens. This spiritual dimension belongs to God (which isn't to say that we won't be able to visit there, etc.). What believers *will* inherit is the earth and the physical universe in which it resides. This is why Peter said redeemed men & women are to be "looking forward to a new heaven and new earth, the *home* of righteousness" (2 Peter 3:13). Once again, the "new heaven" in this text is referring to a new *physical universe* not the spiritual dimension where God's throne is located; although it *could* also be referring to a fusion of these two realms, a possibility we'll consider shortly.

Between Physical Death and Bodily Resurrection

Someone might understandably point out that Paul said "to be absent from the body is to be present with the Lord" (2 Corinthians 5:8). This is why he desired "to depart and be with Christ, which is far better" (Philippians 1:23). These passages show that Christians go to heaven when they die, which is absolutely true. These texts and a few others (e.g. Revelation 6:9-11 & 7:9-17) refer to what theologians call the "intermediate state" of the Christian soul, which pertains to the state of the believer *after* physical death and *before* bodily resurrection. Clearly, the believer will be with the Lord in heaven in a conscious disembodied state, "before the throne of God" and serving him "day and night in his temple" (Revelation 7:15). For details see the article *The Believer's "Intermediate State" (between Physical Death and Bodily resurrection)* at the Fountain of life site.[7]

This shows that there's *some* truth to this notion of "going to heaven" and being in the LORD's presence, but over the centuries it has been blown out of proportion to the extent that the average Christian thinks eternal life is all about spending eternity in an incorporeal state in an ethereal dimension, reclining on a cloud. The more one studies the God-breathed Scriptures, however, the more you realize this simply isn't true. The truth about eternal life is so much more.

There are three important facts about the believer's intermediate state that must be understood:

1. **It's a *temporary* state**—only extending to the aforementioned bodily resurrection or "first resurrection," which takes place in stages, one at the time of Christ's return for his Church (1 Thessalonians 4:13-18), another at the Lord's return to the earth (Revelation 20:4-6) and presumably another at the end of the Millennium. This is covered in chapter 5.
2. **It's an *incomplete* state.** God purposely created the human soul/spirit to dwell in a body (Genesis 2:7, 1 Thessalonians 5:23, etc.). If the disembodied human soul/spirit is fine as is, that would naturally make the bodily resurrection unnecessary, to say the least.

---

[7] Also available in Chapter Ten of the unabridged version of *SHEOL KNOW*.

3. Lastly, **the intermediate state of the Christian soul/spirit in heaven is *de-emphasized* in Scripture**. Other than the passages noted above, you won't read many references to the intermediate state in the Bible. Rather, the bodily resurrection and eternal life are emphasized. For instance, Acts 17:18 shows that Paul preached "the good news of Jesus *and* the resurrection." You see, the resurrection is a fundamental part of the gospel of Christ. For Paul's *"hope in* the resurrection of the dead" he was put on trial (Acts 23:6). What was Paul's hope in, according to this passage? Not the temporary intermediate state, as wonderful as that will be, but the resurrection of the righteous wherein believers receive imperishable, glorified, powerful, spiritual bodies! Read it yourself in 1 Corinthians 15:42-44. More on this in a moment.

So, as wonderful as the believer's intermediate state between physical death and bodily resurrection will be, it's a *temporary* and *incomplete* state that's *de-emphasized* in Scripture, although not ignored. Other than serving in the Lord's presence in heaven in an incorporeal condition, we don't know much about it. It will be a glorious period, for sure, but the impression in Scripture is that this will be a time of anticipation—anticipating our bodily resurrection, anticipating reigning with Christ on this earth for a thousand years, and, most of all, anticipating our everlasting inheritance of the "new heaven and new earth, the home of the righteous" and everything that that involves (2 Peter 3:13).

Quality of Life in the New Earth and Universe

What does the Bible say about this *eternal* age? The quality of life in the new earth & universe will be wholly magnificent, to say the least.

Firstly, the New Jerusalem will be unimaginably huge and glorious: The city will be 1400 miles long and wide (Revelation 21:16). That's approximately the distance from New York City to Wichita, Kansas. Can you imagine a city that immense? It would take a trip of about 6000 miles just to travel around it! What's more, the magnificent golden buildings will extend up into space 1400 miles—these will be skyscrapers indeed! How would you like to live on the top floor?

Revelation 21 describes the city in some detail: The city walls will be made of jasper and will be *200 feet thick*. Each of the huge twelve gates will be made of *a single pearl*. (Where did such huge pearls come from? I don't know. All I can say is there must be a planet out there with some really *big* oysters). The main streets of the city will be pure gold. In fact, the whole city itself will apparently be made of pure gold—so pure it's transparent!

Secondly, notice what the Bible says about our quality of life in the perpetual age-to-come:

> **Now the dwelling of God is with men, and <u>he will live with them</u>. They will be his people, and God Himself <u>will be with them</u> and be their God. ⁴ He will wipe every tear from their eyes. There will be no more death or mourning or crying or pain, for the old order of things has passed away.**
> **Revelation 21:3-4**

We see here that we will be able to see, talk to and walk with God Almighty face to face! This is in perfect harmony with what Jesus Christ said concerning the main characteristic of eternal life:

> "For you [Father God] **granted him** [Jesus] **authority over all people that he might give eternal life to all those you have given him.** ³ <u>Now this is eternal life: that they may know you</u>, the only true God, and Jesus Christ whom you have sent." John 17:2-3

Some suggest that Jesus was defining eternal life here, but this isn't true because 'eternal life' *means* "eternal life." That's its definition. In the Greek the phrase 'eternal life' is *aionios zoe*,[8] which literally means "age-lasting life." Since the age-to-come is a perpetual age scholars usually render *aionios* as "eternal" when used in reference to "eternal life." *Aionios zoe* could also be translated as "the life of the age to come." This is the "abundant" or "full" life Jesus said he came to give people in John 10:10.

Receiving this "life of the age to come" is a two-phase process:

1. Believers receive eternal life in their spirits at the point of spiritual regeneration, which is why the Bible says: "Whoever believes in the Son *has* eternal life [present tense], but whoever rejects the Son will not see life, for God's wrath remains on him" (John 3:36; see also 1 John 5:11-12). The fact that believers presently *have* the abundant life-of-the-age-to-come in their regenerated spirits reveals why it's so important that we learn to put off the "old self"—the flesh—and put on the "new self" (Ephesians 4:22-24). This means living (or walking) in the spirit, not in the flesh. When we do this, **we tap into that full life of God and are able to manifest it in this dark, dying, lost world**.
2. Attaining eternal life is completed at the resurrection of the righteous. This is when we'll receive new imperishable,

---

[8] Pronounced *ay-OH-nee-us ZOH-ay*.

glorified, powerful and spiritual bodies. The fact that the believer's eternal life is *completed* at the bodily resurrection is confirmed by Jesus when he plainly said that believers will receive eternal life "**in** the age to come" (Mark 10:29-30). This is verified by other passages like Titus 1:2, 3:7 and Jude 21.

So, when Christ said "Now this is eternal life: that they may know you," he wasn't defining the life-of-the-age-to-come, **he was emphasizing its most important quality, which is** *knowing God*. Every believer can grow in this quality simply by tapping into the eternal life that's in your spirit, but we have to put off the flesh to do this; it's also necessary to "throw off" every weight or distraction that hinders (Hebrews 12:1). The Bible says, "Come near to God and he will come near to you" (James 4:8). Think about it: We can have as much of God as we want!

Getting back to Revelation 21, verse 4 plainly says that in the era of the new earth & universe there will be no more pain, crying, aging or death—all such maladies will have been eliminated! This makes perfect sense. After all, what good is paradise if one has to suffer pain, aging and death? The passage even says that God Almighty will personally console us regarding the many pains, heartaches and injustices we experienced in our lives in "this present evil age" (Galatians 1:4).

Thirdly, as noted above, the Bible promises new glorified and immortal bodies to those who accept God's gift of eternal life (1 Corinthians 15:42-54). Although we cannot fully comprehend now how wondrous life will be in these new resurrection bodies, we can get an idea simply by observing what the Bible says about Jesus *after* his resurrection. After all, we're going to receive the same type of glorified body he did, that is, *if* you're a believer. In light of this, we'll evidently be able to walk through solid objects (John 20:26), instantly appear out of nowhere and disappear (Luke

24:31,36-37); in other words, we'll be able to *teleport* at will. With this understanding, we'll no doubt be able to take "quantum leaps" to anywhere on the new earth, moon, Mars or universe—*distances and space will no longer limit us.*

For those who argue that Christ is deity and therefore our glorified bodies may not have the same capacity as his, the Bible blatantly says that we are *"co-heirs* with Christ," which means 'joint heirs' or 'joint participants' (Romans 8:17). Besides, why would the LORD reveal to us the incredible abilities of the glorified body through Jesus' actions after his resurrection if the Creator didn't intend for us to have the same incredible capacity when we're bodily resurrected?

Lastly, the text says that "the dwelling of God is with the people, and he will live with them. They will be his people, and God Himself will be with them and be their God" (Revelation 21:3). Since "the dwelling of God" *is* heaven, this seems to suggest some kind of fusion between the spiritual realm (heaven) and the natural realm (earth & universe). As co-heirs with Christ, I'm sure we'll have access to both realms. So perhaps "spending eternity in heaven" is valid in this sense.

There will be Nations and Kings on the New Earth

Additional insights about life in the eternal age-to-come can be observed in this passage:

> I did not see a temple in the city, because the Lord God Almighty and the Lamb are its temple. [23] The city does not need the sun or the moon to shine on it, for the glory of God gives it light, and the Lamb is its lamp. [24] **The nations**

> **will walk by its light**, and **the kings of the earth will bring their splendor into it.** [25] On no day will its gates ever be shut, for there will be no night there [26] The glory and honor of **the nations** will be brought into it.
>
> Revelation 21:22-26

The passage shows that there will be nations of peoples with kings over them on the new earth. The Greek word for "nations" is *ethnos (ETH-nohs)*, meaning "a race, a people or a nation that shares a common and distinctive culture." In short, peoples on the new earth won't be look-alike drones under the supervision of the Most High. Variety is the spice of life, *Praise God!*

Plus there will be kings over these nations; that is, national authorities. And if there are national authorities there will be subordinate authorities, like governors of territories and mayors of cities and so on. Of course, there will also be authority structures in the vast New Jerusalem.

Who will be placed in these authority positions? This parable shows:

> "**Again, it will be like a man going on a journey, who called his servants and entrusted his wealth to them.** [15] **To one he gave five bags of gold, to another two bags, and to another one bag, each according to his ability. Then he went on his journey.** [16] **The man who had received five bags of gold went at once and put his money to work and gained five bags more.** [17] **So also, the one with two bags of gold gained two more.** [18] **But the man who had received one bag went off, dug a hole in the ground and hid his master's money.**

¹⁹ "After a long time the master of those servants returned and settled accounts with them. ²⁰ The man who had received five bags of gold brought the other five. 'Master,' he said, 'you entrusted me with five bags of gold. See, I have gained five more.'

²¹ "His master replied, 'Well done, good and faithful servant! <u>You have been faithful with a few things; I will put you in charge of many things</u>. Come and share your master's happiness!'

²² "The man with two bags of gold also came. 'Master,' he said, 'you entrusted me with two bags of gold; see, I have gained two more.'

²³ "His master replied, 'Well done, good and faithful servant! <u>You have been faithful with a few things; I will put you in charge of many things</u>. Come and share your master's happiness!'

²⁴ "Then the man who had received one bag of gold came. 'Master,' he said, 'I knew that you are a hard man, harvesting where you have not sown and gathering where you have not scattered seed. ²⁵ So I was afraid and went out and hid your gold in the ground. See, here is what belongs to you.'

²⁶ "His master replied, 'You wicked, lazy servant! So you knew that I harvest where I have not sown and gather where I have not scattered seed? ²⁷ Well then, you should have put my money on deposit with the bankers, so that when I returned I would have received it back with interest.

²⁸ "'So take the bag of gold from him and give it to the one who has ten bags. ²⁹ <u>For whoever has will be given more</u>, and they will have an abundance. Whoever does not have, even what they have will be taken from them. ³⁰ And throw that worthless servant outside, into the darkness, where there will be weeping and gnashing of teeth.'

Matthew 25:14-30

The Lord invests in every believer and expects a return on his investment when he returns. The two men in the story who doubled what was invested in them are praised by the master and told, "You have been faithful with a few things; I will put you in charge of many things." This is figurative of the Judgment Seat of Christ, which is the judgment believers undergo (2 Corinthians 5:10-11), as covered last chapter.

Notice how a similar parable puts it:

> "He was made king, however, and returned home. Then he sent for the servants to whom he had given the money, in order to find out what they had gained with it.
> ¹⁶ "The first one came and said, 'Sir, your mina has earned ten more.'
> ¹⁷ " 'Well done, my good servant!' his master replied. '<u>Because you have been trustworthy in a very small matter, take charge of ten cities</u>.'
> ¹⁸ "The second came and said, 'Sir, your mina has earned five more.'
> ¹⁹ "<u>His master answered, 'You take charge of five cities</u>.' "

Luke 19:15-19

The mina was a unit of currency worth three months' wages. The first man was given ten minas and earned ten more while the second man was given five minas and earned five more.

Notice what these men are specifically rewarded with: The first one is put in charge of ten cities and the second five cities.

Both stories are figurative of the literal truth that believers will be rewarded in the coming eternal age according to what they do or don't do with the talents the Lord has invested in them in this current age. Those who are "faithful with a few things" will be "put you in charge of many things." The phrase "put in charge" indicates a position of authority; and the second parable specifies being put in charge of cities.

When and where will faithful believers be put in charge of "many things," including "cities"? On the new earth for sure, but other planets in the new universe as well. I'll offer proof momentarily.

With this understanding, your faithfulness *now* with the few small things the Lord has put you in charge of has eternal ramifications! What has God put you in charge of? Several things: Your body, your mind (thoughts), your family, your job, your Christian service, your money, your talents and the people linked to you, at least as far as your influence goes.

The Entire Universe will be Under Humanity's Control

It goes without saying that living on the paradise of the new earth will be utterly magnificent, but—and this is an important "but"—the new Jerusalem and new earth will only be our **home base**. In other words, *we'll be able to explore and inhabit the unfathomable reaches of the universe!*

We know this for a fact because the Bible doesn't just encourage us to look forward to the new earth as our eternal home of righteousness, but **to the new heavens as well**, which refers to the new universe:

> **But in keeping with his promise <u>we are looking forward to a new heaven and a new earth</u>, the home of righteousness.**
> **2 Peter 3:13**

We are encouraged to look forward to the new universe because it's part of our eternal inheritance, just as much as the new earth is. In fact, the new universe is listed *first*, which gives the impression that we're to look forward to it even more than the new earth. Why? Because *the new earth is merely one planet in an incomprehensibly vast universe!* Now, it might be the most notable planet—since it's our home base—but it's still only one planet amidst gazillions.

Speaking of which, most people don't realize how incredibly vast the universe really is; it's beyond our finite comprehension. To get an idea consider these mind-blowing comparisons: If the thickness of one sheet of paper represented the distance from the Earth to the sun—93 million miles—the distance to the nearest star would be represented by a stack of paper 71 feet high; and the diameter of our Milky Way galaxy would be represented by a stack of paper 310 miles high! To reach the edge of the known universe would take a stack 31 million miles high!

Or consider these awe-inspiring facts: The sun is so huge that if it were hollow, it could hold 1 million earths! The star Antares could contain 64 million suns! There's a star in the constellation Hercules that could contain 100 million 'Antares!' And the largest known star, Epilson, could easily contain several million stars the size of the star in the constellation Hercules! (Kirkwood 374-375).

Don't think for a second that God, our Almighty Creator, formed the incomprehensibly vast universe—the billions of galaxies and incalculable stars & planets for nothing. You can be assured that the *whole universe* will be under humanity's subjection to explore, inhabit, rule, enjoy and who knows what else? As it is written:

> **For You (God) have put everything in subjection under his (humanity's) feet. Now in putting everything in subjection to man, He left nothing outside [of man's] control. But at present we do not yet see all things subjected to him [man].**
> **Hebrews 2:8** (The Amplified Bible)

"Everything" in the physical universe will be put in subjection to redeemed humanity; "everything" will be put in our control. It's interesting to note that 'everything' can also be translated as "the universe," which is how the Weymouth New Testament translates it. Most English versions say "all things." In other words, *nothing in the entire universe will be outside of our control.* As stated above, we will be able to explore, inhabit and rule the unfathomable reaches of the physical universe!

Remember, God originally blessed humankind to "be fruitful and multiply," to "subdue" and "have dominion" over all the earth:

> **And God BLESSED them, and said unto them, "Be fruitful, and multiply, and replenish the earth, and subdue it: and have dominion over the fish of the sea, and over the fowl of the air,**

> **and over every living thing that moveth upon the earth."**
> **Genesis 1:28** (KJV)

This blessing/directive is inherent in the psycho-spiritual DNA of humankind. There's no escaping it; it's our Divine mission; it's part of who we *are*. Unfortunately, the sin nature inevitably twists this blessing and it becomes a curse, resulting in abuse, slavery, wars, environmental raping and so forth. Yet, this doesn't take away from the fact that the intrinsic blessing is wholly *good* and was intended to *empower* humanity to fulfill its Divine mandate—to be fruitful, multiply, replenish, subdue and take dominion. In other words, the LORD didn't create humankind to be servants of the earth, but to be lords over it, which is befitting since Father God is "Lord of heaven and earth," as Jesus Christ Himself acknowledged (Matthew 11:25). Now consider that humanity is created in God's image and believers are called to be "imitators of God" (Ephesians 5:1).

Before I go any further, I want to stress that the LORD doesn't want us to "subdue" and take "dominion" in a negative sense. This needs to be emphasized in light of the fact that people tend to equate "dominion" with carnal control because the devil naturally tries to pervert whatever God creates, commands or blesses. The Creator's mandate was to subdue and hold dominion in LOVE, because "God is love" (1 John 4:7-8,16). This helps make sense of this proverb:

> **<u>Love</u> and <u>faithfulness</u> keep a king safe;**
> **<u>through</u> <u>love</u> his throne is made secure.**
> **Proverbs 20:28**

A "king" refers to an authority figure. In our day and age it would apply to anyone who has authority in any given environment: a father or mother, a teacher or professor, an employer or supervisor, a president or governor, a pastor or apostle, a police officer or security guard, etc. This proverb reveals the godly way of keeping one's position of authority—one's "throne"—safe and secure: **through love and faithfulness**. So, when the Bible talks about "subduing" and taking "dominion" it's talking about doing so in love and faithfulness, not being an abusive tyrant. Are you with me?

Now, here's something interesting: The Garden of Eden was roughly the size of California or Iraq according to the specifications cited in the Bible and some guesswork (Genesis 2:8-14[9]). It was already a paradise, which is the way God created it, but the rest of the earth wasn't. The rest of the planet had potential, but it was untamed and uncultivated, which is why the LORD empowered humankind to subdue it and take dominion. In other words, God blessed humanity to make the rest of the planet the same paradise as that of the Garden of Eden, which is why Genesis 1:28 above twice stresses replenishing and subduing "the earth" and not the Garden of Eden since the latter was already replenished and subdued.

The paradise of the Garden of Eden was God's blueprint for humankind to expand on until the entire planet was a paradise. Once 'Project Earth' was completed they could go on to subdue and replenish every planet in the solar system, the galaxy, and ultimately the furthest reaches of the universe! Why do you think all those innumerable barren planets are there for? They're there for us to reach and subdue, in love and faithfulness. This is supported by Hebrews 2:8 above: God has placed *"everything"* in

---

[9] The NKJV renders verse 8 as "The LORD God planted <u>a garden **eastward** in Eden</u>, and there He put the man whom He had formed." If "eastward" was in relation to where Moses was when he wrote Genesis, then it likely refers to the Mesopotamian Valley, which is approximately the size of California or Iraq.

the natural universe in subjection to humanity—*"nothing"* is outside of redeemed humanity's control! Chew on that.

Doesn't this remind you of various science-fiction shows, films and books—humanity uniting together and going out to the furthest reaches of space to peaceably explore and inhabit? Star Trek is the most obvious example. The visionaries of these sci-fi works are people created in God's image who instinctively grasp the Creator's blessing/directive because it's part of our spiritual DNA. The significant difference in the biblical model is that there will be no pain, hostility, war, disease, aging or death, not to mention the presence of the Almighty. All humanity will truly be united together in love, mutual respect and acceptance under the perfectly just govern-ship of the Creator of All.

Aging and death are the ailments that taint the optimistic visions of these sci-fi works the most. After all, what good is envisioning such a grand future for humanity and all living beings if we're dead and not able to see it? And even if we were to live in the distant era depicted in these works, no matter how utopian it might be, we'd all still ultimately succumb to the universal curse of aging and death.

But, Praise God, the glorious gospel settles this problem; believers escape death through the death & resurrection of Jesus Christ, reconciling with the Almighty and attaining immortality and eternal life (2 Timothy 1:10)!

Where the Error Started

As you can see, the Bible is very explicit concerning *where* redeemed people will spend eternal life. Genuine theologians will agree with this biblical data but you'll rarely hear these fascinating scriptural facts taught in Christian circles. More likely you'll hear it all condensed to "spending eternity in heaven," which, again, gives the impression of sprouting wings and living in an ethereal dimension forever, lazily strumming a harp on a cloud or whatever. This is the *religious* version of the wonderful truths of God's Word, the *counterfeit* version. Needless to say, the religious version isn't invigorating; it isn't interesting. It's too fantastical and one-dimensional. In a word, it's *boring*.

This misleading religious error can be traced to Augustine of Hippo (354-430 AD), one of the most influential theologians in Christian history. Unfortunately, Augustine was strongly influenced by Greek philosophy, a belief system that viewed the physical universe, including the body, as evil. Consequently, the biblical teaching that redeemed people will spend eternity in glorified *bodies* in a *literal* New Jerusalem on a *literal* new earth in a *tangible* new universe was a blasphemous concept. Augustine solved this problem by *spiritualizing* what the Bible plainly taught, suggesting that biblical references like "the new Jerusalem" and "new earth" are merely symbolic language for heaven. This is how the false doctrine of amillennialism developed.[10] His views were officially accepted by the Council of Ephesus in 431 AD and are held by many professing Christians today. This doesn't mean that they're not legitimate believers, of course, just that they're ignorant of what the Bible plainly teaches on the nature of eternal life. What a testimony to the formidable, blinding force of religious tradition and indoctrination!

This, by the way, explains my purpose in including this chapter on eternal life in this book—to set the captives FREE.

---

[10] See the corresponding article at the Fountain of Life site for details. Chapters Seven and Nine of the unabridged version of *HELL KNOW* also address this issue.

The Coming Universal Utopia

So, according to the biblical scriptures, what these sci-fi luminaries write about in their fictional works *will* essentially come to pass: humanity *will* indeed unite together to peaceably explore and inhabit the far reaches of the universe, but we'll be free of the maladies that forever mar their stories—evil, pain, disease, aging and death.

Unfortunately, it's going to get worse before it gets better, as detailed in chapters 5 and 6. The Bible promises a 7-year Tribulation for humanity and the earth before the establishment of the new earth and universe, not to mention a great judgment wherein all humanity will be divinely judged; those who rejected reconciliation with their Creator will suffer the "second death" which is described as "everlasting destruction" (2 Thessalonians 1:9 & Revelation 20:11-15). Why must this happen? Because of the axiom: "The wages of sin is death"; thankfully, the passage goes on to say "but the gift of God is eternal life in Christ Jesus our Lord" (Romans 6:23). This is the 'good news.'

Allow me to stress that Christianity is not a legalistic drudgery, as those steeped in life-stifling religiosity give the impression. At its core Christianity is an exciting *relationship* with the Creator of the universe, which is why the gospel is referred to as "the message of *reconciliation*" in the Bible (2 Corinthians 5:18-19). The primary purpose of the 'good news' is to reconcile people to their Maker (Romans 5:10-11). Immortality in the new earth & universe is merely a byproduct of this reconciliation or, we could say, "icing on the cake."

The most popular verse in the Bible says "For God so loved the world that he gave his one and only Son, that whoever believes in him shall not perish but have eternal life" (John 3:16). God is clearly extending his love to all humanity and definitely wants *everyone* to accept His gracious offer of eternal life. As we have seen, this "eternal life" does not consist of lying on a cloud playing a harp forever as religion has erroneously told us; no, it's far more invigorating, far more purposeful and far more adventurous. In fact, the Scriptures state that, "No eye has seen, no ear has heard, no mind has conceived what God has prepared for those who love him" (1 Corinthians 2:9). The nature of our existence in the new universe will be so awe-inspiringly wonderful that it's presently beyond our finite comprehension! The biblical descriptions we've witnessed in this chapter are but a "poor reflection as in a mirror" (1 Corinthians 13:12). In other words, we're seeing solid pieces of the truth, but they're only the tip of the iceberg. Praise the Lord!

"The Final Restoration of All Things"

The awesome news is that creation will be redeemed and, in fact, *yearns* for it:

> **For the creation waits <u>in eager expectation</u> for the children of God to be revealed.**
> **Romans 8:19**

What does creation wait in eager expectation for? The children of God to be revealed, which is part of the "restoration of all things":

> **For he [Christ] must remain in heaven until the time for <u>the final restoration of all things</u>, as God promised long ago through his holy prophets.**
> **Acts 3:21**

This restoration of all things takes place in stages. One key stage is when Jesus returns for his Church wherein believers' bodies are finally redeemed:

> **We know that <u>the whole creation has been groaning as in the pains of childbirth right up to the present time</u>.** [23] **Not only so, but we ourselves, who have the firstfruits of the Spirit, groan inwardly as we wait eagerly for our adoption to sonship, <u>the redemption of our bodies</u>.**
> **Romans 8:22-23**

Christ's return for the Church is the Rapture and is detailed in 1 Thessalonians 4:13-18, covered in chapter 5.

This restoration continues after the 7-year Tribulation when Jesus returns to earth and establishes his millennial kingdom. Tribulation martyrs and Old Testament saints will be resurrected at this time and the lifespans of mortal humans—those determined "sheep" in the Sheep and Goat Judgment, covered in chapter 6—will return to the lengthy lifespans of people before the flood.

Isaiah 11:6-9 shows what life will be like during the Millennium: Carnivorous animals will become herbivorous and therefore wolves will live with lambs and leopards will lie together with goats; calves and lions will hang out and be led by little children. Cows and bears will feed together and formerly carnivorous beasts like the lion will eat straw like an ox. Furthermore, children will play by the cobra's den and by the viper's nest without fear because poisonous creatures will no longer be poisonous.

What's the Purpose of the Millennium?

The Millennium is the LORD's irrefutable proof to humanity that the religion of secular humanism is a lie. As you may or may not know, secular humanism is atheistic in nature and therefore anti-God. To those who embrace this godless religion there's no sin problem because there's no God with whom to sin against. To them, the problem of evil isn't humanity's sin nature and alienation from our Creator, but rather a negative environment. As such, they believe evil, crime, poverty, war and other ailments will largely be eradicated when the right government is in place and every person is provided an education, a decent job, a nice living environment, protection from crime, and so on. While these things are good they don't actually remedy the sin problem or reconcile people to their Creator. After all, a white collar man living in a rich suburb is still perfectly able to commit fraud due to a greedy heart, not to mention be a drunkard, drug addict, wife-beater, slanderer, hypocrite, adulterer, murderer, blowhard, oppressor, porn addict, pedophile or practicing homosexual.

In the Millennium the LORD is going to provide nations of mortals the perfect government and environment—a veritable worldwide utopia. Since Jesus will be the King over all the earth and his assistants will be glorified believers who don't have a sin nature there will be zero corruption in the government (imagine that!). Yet as the population increases over the course of the Millennium many of the offspring of the original "sheep" will just go through the motions of being faithful to Christ while their hearts aren't in it. This is legalism—putting on the airs of godliness without the heart of godliness. Because legalism is an "outward job" it's decidedly inauthentic. As such, when the devil is unleashed at the end of the thousand years these covert rebels will naturally embrace the lies of the kingdom of darkness and unite for war in an insane attempt to take over the completely righteous government of Christ!

Of course the rebellion is quickly quelled (Revelation 20:9) and, after the Great White Throne Judgment, the eternal age of the new heavens and new earth will manifest (Revelation 21-22).

So the Millennium is the Most High's eternal showcase in disproving the religion of secular humanism. Chew on that!

Conclusion on the Final Restoration of All Things

As wonderful as the thousand-year reign of Christ will be, it's just another stage in the "restoration of all things." The final stage takes place when God wholly renovates the earth & universe and the heavenly city, the New Jerusalem, will come "down out of heaven from God" to rest on the new earth, as detailed earlier.

The Greek word for 'restoration' in the phrase "the final restoration of all things" is *apokatastasis (ap-ok-at-AS-tas-is)*, which appears only once in the Bible, Acts 3:21. The root word is *apokathistémi (ap-ok-ath-IS-tay-mee)*, which means "to set up again" and "restore to its original position or condition." That's what the "restoration of all things" is about—restoring humanity, the earth and universe to their original condition before the fall, which is the way God originally intended it to be.

The Messiah spoke of this restoration in this passage:

> **Jesus said to them, "Truly I tell you, at <u>the renewal of all things</u>, when the Son of Man sits on his glorious throne, you who have followed**

> me will also sit on twelve thrones, judging the twelve tribes of Israel."
>
> Matthew 19:28

The Greek word for 'renewal' here is *paliggenesia (pal-ing-ghen-es-EE-ah)*, which means "new birth, regeneration or renewal." It's only used twice in Scripture. The second time is in Titus 3:5 where it refers to the **regeneration** *of the human spirit* when a believer accepts the gospel (John 3:3,6). This shows that the "renewal of all things" is actually being jump-started in this current age through the spiritual rebirth of believers. This culminates with Christ's return for his Church, detailed above. The next stage of the "renewal" takes place when Christ returns to the earth to establish his millennial reign, which is what Jesus was specifically referring to in the above passage, Matthew 19:28. This renewal climaxes with the renovation of the new heavens and new earth, the eternal age to come.

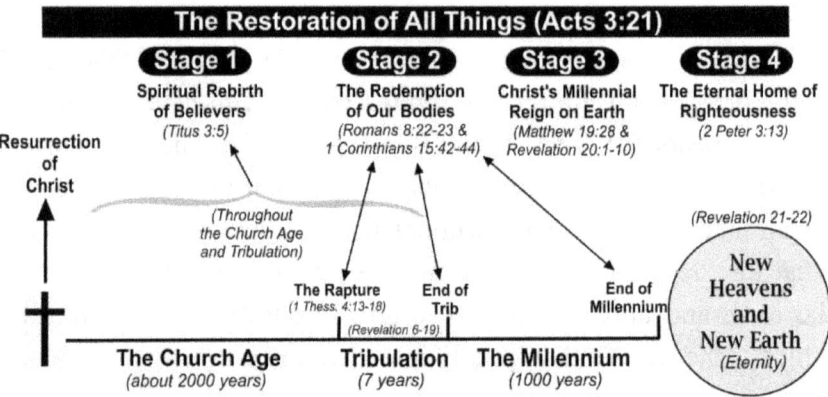

I want to stress that the animal kingdom and even the plant kingdom are partakers in this redemption of the physical universe. Why else would all creation "wait in eager expectation" for this great restoration if they were not included in it (Romans 8:19)? This of course doesn't mean animals and trees are literally yearning for this renewal, but they yearn for it in a figurative sense because *they're included in it.*

David Reagan shared an interesting insight on his TV program, Christ in Prophecy: When the high priest sprinkled animal blood on the cover of the Ark of the Covenant once a year to atone for the sins of the Israelites, this blood covered God's Law, which was represented in the Ark via the tablets of the Ten Commandments. This ritual resulted in God's mercy year to year, covering the Israelites' sins. But the blood of animals could only temporarily cover sin, not cleanse it away forever (Hebrews 10:1-4). The good news is that Jesus Christ, who is the believer's High Priest, offered his own blood when he went to the Most Holy Place in heaven, not merely the blood of animals (Hebrews 9:23-28).

Leviticus 16:15 shows the high priest sprinkling blood on the ground in front of the Ark after sprinkling it on the cover. At the time, the Ark was housed in the tent tabernacle and so the blood was literally poured on the ground. Why is this significant? Because the entire ceremony pointed to Christ's blood atonement in heaven and the priest didn't just sprinkle blood on the lid of the Ark for the redemption of humanity, but also on the ground for the redemption of all physical creation.

Were there animals before the fall? Yes. Therefore there will be animals after the fall; that is, in the eternal age-to-come. The question is, will the LORD create new animals or will he simply resurrect animals that have already lived and died? Or both?

Eternity and Your Beloved Pets

While animals are not created in the image of God, the same Hebrew and Greek words for "soul" are used in reference to animals in the Scriptures. *Nephesh (neh-FESH)* is the Hebrew word for "soul" whereas *psuche (soo-KHAY)* is the corresponding Greek word. Observe how these words are used for animals:

- "let the water teem with living **creatures** *(nephesh)*" and "let the land produce living **creatures** *(nephesh)*" - Genesis 1:20,24
- "…every living **thing** *(psuche)* in the sea died" - Revelation 16:3

My point? Every animal has a soulish DNA and thus God can resurrect any creature he wants in the eternal age-to-come. People naturally wonder about their beloved pets and animals. Will they ever see them again? Will they be reunited with them in the new heavens and new earth? While the Scriptures don't directly address the question, the answer is obvious based on several passages. For instance, how could it be the "restoration of all things" if one's beloved pets are omitted? If Jesus said we are to ask and receive so our joy might be complete on this imperfect earth (John 16:24), how much more so on the new earth, which will be perfect? Doesn't the Bible say that those who delight themselves in the LORD will receive the desires of their hearts (Psalm 37:4)? If this is so in this wicked age, how much more so in the righteous age to come? Really, it's just common sense.

Are You Looking Forward to Eternal Life?

This chapter is just a taste of what we have to look forward to in the eternal age of the new heavens and new earth. Are you excited? *I am!*

Conclusion

I encourage you to master the six basic doctrines of Christianity. Those who do so set a solid foundation for their spiritual walk, which protects them from life-stifling legalism, feeble quasi-spirituality and false doctrine, including dubious traditional doctrines.

May the LORD bless you in your service as you continue to seek and apply what you learn.

Amen and Amen.

Bibliography

Brown, Francis/Driver, S.R./Briggs, Charles A. *Brown-Driver-Briggs Lexicon.* Peabody: Hendrickson Publishers, 1994

Bullinger, Ethelbert W. *A Critical Lexicon and Concordance to the English and Greek New Testament.* Grand Rapids: Zondervan Publishing House, 1975

Helps Word-Studies Lexicon. Retrieved from Biblehub.com. 1987, 2011

Lindsey, Hal. There's a New World Coming. New York: Bantam Books, 1973

Kirkwood, David. *Your Best Year Yet!* Pittsburgh: Ethnos Press, 1996

LORD, The. *Berean Study Bible (BSB).* Bible Hub, 2016

LORD, The. *English Standard Version (ESV). Holy Bible.* Chicago: Crossway, 2001

LORD, The. *Good News Translation. Holy Bible.* The Bible Society, 2001

LORD, The. *International Standard Version. Holy Bible.* Davidson Press, 1999

LORD, The. *King James Version. Holy Bible.* Iowa Falls: World Bible Publishers

LORD, The. *New American Standard Bible. Holy Bible.* Nashville: Holman, 1977

LORD, The. *New International Version. Holy Bible.* Nashville: Holman, 1986

LORD, The. *New International Version (Revised). Holy Bible.* Nashville: Holman, 2011

LORD, The. *New King James Version Study Bible: Second Edition.* Nashville: Thomas Nelson, 2012

LORD, The. *New Living Translation*. Carol Stream: Tyndale House Publishers, 2006

LORD, The. New Revised Standard Version. Holy Bible. Nashville: Nelson, 1989

LORD, The. *The Amplified Bible*. Grand Rapids: Zondervan, 1987

LORD, The. *Quest Study Bible: New International Version*. Grand Rapids: Zondervan, 2003

LORD, The. *World English Bible (WEB)*. Salt Lake City: Project Gutenberg, 2013

LORD, The. *Weymouth New Testament*. Ulan Press, 2012

LORD, The. *Young's Literal Translation (YLT)*. Grand Rapids: Baker Books, 1989

Savelle, Jerry. *In the Footsteps of a Prophet*. Crowley: Jerry Savelle Publications, 1999

Strandberg, Todd. Defending the Pre-Trib Rapture. Retrieved from https://www.raptureready.com/rr-pre-trib-rapture.html

Strong, James. *Strong's Exhaustive Concordance*. Grand Rapids: Baker, 1991

Vine, W.E. *Vine's Expository Dictionary of Biblical Words*. Cambridge: Nelson, 1985

Fountain of Life
Teaching Ministry
(Psalm 36:9)

The mission of Fountain of Life is to **set the captives FREE** by **reaching the world** with the **life-changing truths of God's Word**, the **power of the Holy Spirit** and the **Awesome News of the message of Jesus Christ**.

We're calling Spiritual Warriors all over the Earth to partner with us on this mission!

Books by Dirk Waren:

The Believer's Guide to Forgiveness & Warfare
Legalism Unmasked
HELL KNOW!
SHEOL KNOW!
The Four Stages of Spiritual Growth
ANGELS: Their Purpose and Your Responsibility
THE LAW and the Believer
The SIX BASIC DOCTRINES of Christianity

www.ingramcontent.com/pod-product-compliance
Lightning Source LLC
Chambersburg PA
CBHW060506030426
42337CB00015B/1767

Business Fables Adapted From Aesop For Humans Who Work For a Living

Erika Schelby

LAVA GATE PRESS

Copyright © 2022 Erika Schelby

All rights reserved.

ISBN 978-0-9891216-4-4